MznLnx

Missing Links Exam Preps

Exam Prep for

Marketing

Grewal & Levy, 1st Edition

The MznLnx Exam Prep is your link from the texbook and lecture to your exams.
The MznLnx Exam Preps are unauthorized and comprehensive reviews of your textbooks.

MznLnx

Rico
Publications

Exam Prep for Marketing
1st Edition
Grewal & Levy

Publisher: Raymond Houge
Assistant Editor: Michael Rouger
Text and Cover Designer: Lisa Buckner
Marketing Manager: Sara Swagger
Project Manager, Editorial Production: Jerry Emerson
Art Director: Vernon Lowerui
Product Manager: Dave Mason
Editorial Assitant: Rachel Guzmanji
Pedagogy: Debra Long
Cover Image: Jim Reed/Getty Images
Text and Cover Printer: City Printing, Inc.
Compositor: Media Mix, Inc.

Printed in the United States
ISBN:

For more information about our products, contact us at:
Dave.Mason@RicoPublications.com

For permission to use material from this text or product, submit a request online to:
Dave.Mason@RicoPublications.com

Contents

TO THE STUDENT

COMPREHENSIVE

The *MznLnx* Exam Prep series is designed to help you pass your exams. Editors at MznLnx review your textbooks and then prepare these practice exams to help you master the textbook material. Unlike study guides, workbooks, and practice tests provided by the texbook publisher and textbook authors, *MznLnx* gives you ***all*** of the material in each chapter in exam form, not just samples, so you can be sure to nail your exam.

MECHANICAL

The MznLnx Exam Prep series creates exams that will help you learn the subject matter as well as test you on your understanding. Each question is designed to help you master the concept. Just working through the exams, you gain an understanding of the subject--its a simple mechanical process that produces success.

INTEGRATED STUDY GUIDE AND REVIEW

MznLnx is not just a set of exams designed to test you, its also a comprehensive review of the subject content. Each exam question is also a review of the concept, making sure that you will get the answer correct without having to go to other sources of material. You learn as you go! Its the easiest way to pass an exam.

HUMOR

Studying can be tedious and dry. MznLnx's instructional design includes moderate humor within the exam questions on occassion, to break the tedium and revitalize the brain

1. The _________ is a professional association for marketers. As of 2008 it had approximately 40,000 members. There are collegiate chapters on 250 campuses.

a. ACNielsen
b. AMAX
c. ADTECH
d. American Marketing Association

2. _________ is defined by the American _________ Association as the activity, set of institutions, and processes for creating, communicating, delivering, and exchanging offerings that have value for customers, clients, partners, and society at large. The term developed from the original meaning which referred literally to going to market, as in shopping, or going to a market to sell goods or services.

_________ practice tends to be seen as a creative industry, which includes advertising, distribution and selling.

a. Marketing myopia
b. Customer acquisition management
c. Product naming
d. Marketing

3. A _________ is a written document that details the necessary actions to achieve one or more marketing objectives. It can be for a product or service, a brand, or a product line. _________s cover between one and five years.

a. Prosumer
b. Disruptive technology
c. Marketing strategy
d. Marketing plan

4. The _________ is generally accepted as the use and specification of the four p's describing the strategic position of a product in the marketplace. One version of the origins of the _________ starts in 1948 when James Culliton said that a marketing decision should be a result of something similar to a recipe. This version continued in 1953 when Neil Borden, in his American Marketing Association presidential address, took the recipe idea one step further and coined the term 'Marketing-Mix'.

a. Power III
b. 180SearchAssistant
c. 6-3-5 Brainwriting
d. Marketing mix

5. In business and engineering, new _________ is the term used to describe the complete process of bringing a new product or service to market. There are two parallel paths involved in the Nproduct development process: one involves the idea generation, product design, and detail engineering; the other involves market research and marketing analysis. Companies typically see new _________ as the first stage in generating and commercializing new products within the overall strategic process of product life cycle management used to maintain or grow their market share.

a. New product screening
b. Specification tree
c. New product development
d. Product development

6. _________ deals with the first of the '4P''s of marketing, which are Product, Pricing, Place, and Promotion. _________, as opposed to product management, deals with more outbound marketing tasks. For example, product management deals with the nuts and bolts of product development within a firm, whereas _________ deals with marketing the product to prospects, customers, and others.

a. Reverse hierarchy
b. Corporate transparency
c. Crisis management
d. Product Marketing

7. _________ is an advertisement in which a particular product specifically mentions a competitor by name for the express purpose of showing why the competitor is inferior to the product naming it.

This should not be confused with parody advertisements, where a fictional product is being advertised for the purpose of poking fun at the particular advertisement, nor should it be confused with the use of a coined brand name for the purpose of comparing the product without actually naming an actual competitor. ('Wikipedia tastes better and is less filling than the Encyclopedia Galactica.')

In the 1980s, during what has been referred to as the cola wars, soft-drink manufacturer Pepsi ran a series of advertisements where people, caught on hidden camera, in a blind taste test, chose Pepsi over rival Coca-Cola.

a. GL-70
b. Heavy-up
c. Comparative advertising
d. Cost per conversion

8. A _________ or logistics network is the system of organizations, people, technology, activities, information and resources involved in moving a product or service from supplier to customer. _________ activities transform natural resources, raw materials and components into a finished product that is delivered to the end customer. In sophisticated _________ systems, used products may re-enter the _________ at any point where residual value is recyclable.

a. Supply chain network
b. Supply chain
c. Demand chain management
d. Purchasing

9. In operant conditioning, _________ occurs when an event following a response causes an increase in the probability of that response occurring in the future. Response strength can be assessed by measures such as the frequency with which the response is made (for example, a pigeon may peck a key more times in the session), or the speed with which it is made (for example, a rat may run a maze faster.) The environment change contingent upon the response is called a reinforcer.

a. Completely randomized designs
b. Relationship Management Application
c. Generic brands
d. Reinforcement

10. _________ in economics and business is the result of an exchange and from that trade we assign a numerical monetary value to a good, service or asset. If I trade 4 apples for an orange, the _________ of an orange is 4 - apples. Inversely, the _________ of an apple is 1/4 oranges.

a. Pricing
b. Contribution margin-based pricing
c. Discounts and allowances
d. Price

11. A personal and cultural _________ is a relative ethic _________, an assumption upon which implementation can be extrapolated. A _________ system is a set of consistent _________s and measures that is soo not true. A principle _________ is a foundation upon which other _________s and measures of integrity are based.

a. Value
b. Perceptual maps
c. Package-on-Package
d. Supreme Court of the United States

12. _________ , according to The American Marketing Association, is 'a planning process designed to assure that all brand contacts received by a customer or prospect for a product, service, or organization are relevant to that person and consistent over time.' (Marketing Power Dictionary)

_________ is a term used to describe a holistic approach to marketing. It aims to ensure consistency of message and the complementary use of media. The concept includes online and offline marketing channels.

a. ACNielsen
b. Integrated marketing communications
c. AMAX
d. ADTECH

13. _________ involves disseminating information about a product, product line, brand, or company. It is one of the four key aspects of the marketing mix. (The other three elements are product marketing, pricing, and distribution). P>_________ is generally sub-divided into two parts:

- Above the line _________: Promotion in the media (e.g. TV, radio, newspapers, Internet and Mobile Phones) in which the advertiser pays an advertising agency to place the ad
- Below the line _________: All other _________. Much of this is intended to be subtle enough for the consumer to be unaware that _________ is taking place. E.g. sponsorship, product placement, endorsements, sales _________, merchandising, direct mail, personal selling, public relations, trade shows

a. Promotion
b. Cashmere Agency
c. Davie Brown Index
d. Bottling lines

14. _________ is a broad label that refers to any individuals or households that use goods and services generated within the economy. The concept of a _________ is used in different contexts, so that the usage and significance of the term may vary.

A _________ is a person who uses any product or service.

a. 180SearchAssistant
b. 6-3-5 Brainwriting
c. Power III
d. Consumer

15. _________ is the study of when, why, how, where and what people do or do not buy products. It blends elements from psychology, sociology,social psychology, anthropology and economics. It attempts to understand the buyer decision making process, both individually and in groups. It studies characteristics of individual consumers such as demographics and behavioural variables in an attempt to understand people's wants. It also tries to assess influences on the consumer from groups such as family, friends, reference groups, and society in general.

a. Multidimensional scaling
b. Communal marketing
c. Consumer confidence
d. Consumer behavior

16. _________ refers to messages and related media used to communicate with a market. Those who practice advertising, branding, direct marketing, graphic design, marketing, packaging, promotion, publicity, sponsorship, public relations, sales, sales promotion and online marketing are termed marketing communicators, _________ managers, or more briefly as marcom managers.

a. Merchandising
b. Merchandise
c. Sales promotion
d. Marketing communication

17. A _________, in marketing, procurement, and organizational studies, is a group of employees, family members, or members of any type of organization responsible for purchasing an item for the organization. In a business setting, major purchases typically require input from various parts of the organization, including finance, accounting, purchasing, information technology management, and senior management. Highly technical purchases, such as information systems or production equipment, also require the expertise of technical specialists.

a. Marketing myopia
b. Commercialization
c. Buying center
d. Packshot

18. _________ is the practice of individuals including commercial businesses, governments and institutions, facilitating the sale of their products or services to other companies or organizations that in turn resell them, use them as components in products or services they offer _________ is also called business-to-_________ for short. (Note that while marketing to government entities shares some of the same dynamics of organizational marketing, B2G Marketing is meaningfully different.)

a. Disruptive technology
b. Mass marketing
c. Law of disruption
d. Business marketing

19. _________, or Value optimized pricing is a business strategy. It sets selling prices on the perceived value to the customer, rather than on the actual cost of the product, the market price, competitors prices, or the historical price.

The goal of _________ is to align price with value delivered.

a. Value-based pricing
b. Money back guarantee
c. Jobbing house
d. Service-profit chain

20. A _________ is a collection of symbols, experiences and associations connected with a product, a service, a person or any other artifact or entity.

_________s have become increasingly important components of culture and the economy, now being described as 'cultural accessories and personal philosophies'.

Some people distinguish the psychological aspect of a _________ from the experiential aspect.

a. Brand equity
b. Brandable software
c. Store brand
d. Brand

21. _________ is a rivalry between individuals, groups, nations for territory, a niche, or allocation of resources. It arises whenever two or more parties strive for a goal which cannot be shared. _________ occurs naturally between living organisms which co-exist in the same environment.

a. Price competition
b. Non-price competition
c. Competition
d. Price fixing

22. _________ is a measure of the strength of a brand, product, service relative to competitive offerings. There is often a geographic element to the competitive landscape. In defining _________, you must see to what extent a product, brand, or firm controls a product category in a given geographic area.

a. Discretionary spending
b. Market system
c. Productivity
d. Market dominance

23. In economics, business, retail, and accounting, a _________ is the value of money that has been used up to produce something, and hence is not available for use anymore. In economics, a _________ is an alternative that is given up as a result of a decision. In business, the _________ may be one of acquisition, in which case the amount of money expended to acquire it is counted as _________.

a. Fixed costs
b. Variable cost
c. Transaction cost
d. Cost

24. In economics, _________ is the desire to own something and the ability to pay for it. The term _________ signifies the ability or the willingness to buy a particular commodity at a given point of time .

.

a. Discretionary spending
b. Market dominance
c. Market system
d. Demand

25. In economics, the _________ can be defined as the graph depicting the relationship between the price of a certain commodity, and the amount of it that consumers are willing and able to purchase at that given price. It is a graphic representation of a demand schedule The _________ for all consumers together follows from the _________ of every individual consumer: the individual demands at each price are added together.

_________s are used to estimate behaviors in competitive markets, and are often combined with supply curves to estimate the equilibrium price (the price at which sellers together are willing to sell the same amount as buyers together are willing to buy, also known as market clearing price) and the equilibrium quantity (the amount of that good or service that will be produced and bought without surplus/excess supply or shortage/excess demand) of that market.

a. Power III
b. 6-3-5 Brainwriting
c. Demand curve
d. 180SearchAssistant

26. _________ is one of the four Ps of the marketing mix. The other three aspects are product, promotion, and place. It is also a key variable in microeconomic price allocation theory.

a. Price
b. Competitor indexing
c. Pricing
d. Relationship based pricing

27. _________ consists of the processes a company uses to track and organize its contacts with its current and prospective customers. _________ software is used to support these processes; information about customers and customer interactions can be entered, stored and accessed by employees in different company departments. Typical _________ goals are to improve services provided to customers, and to use customer contact information for targeted marketing.

a. Demand generation
b. Commercialization
c. Product bundling
d. Customer relationship management

28. _________ in its literal sense is the process of transformation of local or regional phenomena into global ones. It can be described as a process by which the people of the world are unified into a single society and function together.

This process is a combination of economic, technological, sociocultural and political forces.

a. 180SearchAssistant
b. 6-3-5 Brainwriting
c. Power III
d. Globalization

29. Customer _________ consists of the processes a company uses to track and organize its contacts with its current and prospective customers. CRelationship management software is used to support these processes; information about customers and customer interactions can be entered, stored and accessed by employees in different company departments. Typical CRelationship management goals are to improve services provided to customers, and to use customer contact information for targeted marketing.

a. Marketing
b. Product bundling
c. Green marketing
d. Relationship management

30. _________ or _________ data refers to selected population characteristics as used in government, marketing or opinion research, or the _________ profiles used in such research. Note the distinction from the term 'demography' Commonly-used _________ include race, age, income, disabilities, mobility (in terms of travel time to work or number of vehicles available), educational attainment, home ownership, employment status, and even location.

a. Demographic
b. AStore
c. Albert Einstein
d. African Americans

31. _________ is a cohort which consists of those people born after the Generation X cohort. Its name is controversial and is synonymous with several alternative names including The Net Generation, Millennials, Echo Boomers, and iGeneration. _________ consists primarily of the offspring of the Generation Jones and Baby Boomers cohorts.

a. AStore
b. Generation Y
c. Greatest Generation
d. Generation X

32. _________ is a contract between two parties, one being the employer and the other being the employee. An employee may be defined as: 'A person in the service of another under any contract of hire, express or implied, oral or written, where the employer has the power or right to control and direct the employee in the material details of how the work is to be performed.' Black's Law Dictionary page 471 (5th ed. 1979.)

a. ADTECH
b. ACNielsen
c. AMAX
d. Employment

33. Importance of _________ is critical for any commercial organization. Expanding business is not possible without increasing sales volumes, and effective _________ goal is to organize sales team work in such a manner that ensures a growing flow of regular customers and increasing amount of sales.

The four phase-model of Management Process

1. Conception
2. Planning
3. Execution
4. Control

This model is cyclical, so it is a constant/continuous process.

===_________ is attainment of sales force goals in a effective ' efficient manner through planning, staffing, training, leading ' controlling organizational resources.

a. Hit rate
b. Sales process
c. Sales management
d. Request for proposal

34. An _________ is a person who has possession of an enterprise and assumes significant accountability for the inherent risks and the outcome. It is an ambitious leader who combines land, labour, and capital to create and market new goods or services. The term is a loanword from French and was first defined by the Irish economist Richard Cantillon.

a. ADTECH
b. AMAX
c. ACNielsen
d. Entrepreneur

35. _________ is the practice of starting new organizations or revitalizing mature organizations, particularly new businesses generally in response to identified opportunities. _________ is often a difficult undertaking, as a vast majority of new businesses fail. Entrepreneurial activities are substantially different depending on the type of organization that is being started.

a. ADTECH
b. AMAX
c. ACNielsen
d. Entrepreneurship

36. _________ is a form of communication that typically attempts to persuade potential customers to purchase or to consume more of a particular brand of product or service. 'While now central to the contemporary global economy and the reproduction of global production networks, it is only quite recently that _________ has been more than a marginal influence on patterns of sales and production. The formation of modern _________ was intimately bound up with the emergence of new forms of monopoly capitalism around the end of the 19th and beginning of the 20th century as one element in corporate strategies to create, organize and where possible control markets, especially for mass produced consumer goods.

a. ADTECH
b. Advertising
c. ACNielsen
d. AMAX

37. _________ is the ability of an individual or group to seclude themselves or information about themselves and thereby reveal themselves selectively. The boundaries and content of what is considered private differ among cultures and individuals, but share basic common themes. _________ is sometimes related to anonymity, the wish to remain unnoticed or unidentified in the public realm.

a. 6-3-5 Brainwriting
b. Power III
c. Privacy
d. 180SearchAssistant

38. According to the American Marketing Association, _________ is the marketing of products that are presumed to be environmentally safe. Thus _________ incorporates a broad range of activities, including product modification, changes to the production process, packaging changes, as well as modifying advertising. Yet defining _________ is not a simple task where several meanings intersect and contradict each other; an example of this will be the existence of varying social, environmental and retail definitions attached to this term.

a. Value proposition
b. Green marketing
c. Commercialization
d. Customer Interaction Tracker

1. A _________ is a process that can allow an organization to concentrate its limited resources on the greatest opportunities to increase sales and achieve a sustainable competitive advantage. A _________ should be centered around the key concept that customer satisfaction is the main goal.

A _________ is most effective when it is an integral component of corporate strategy, defining how the organization will successfully engage customers, prospects, and competitors in the market arena.

a. Psychographic
b. Cyberdoc
c. Societal marketing
d. Marketing strategy

2. _________ is defined by the American _________ Association as the activity, set of institutions, and processes for creating, communicating, delivering, and exchanging offerings that have value for customers, clients, partners, and society at large. The term developed from the original meaning which referred literally to going to market, as in shopping, or going to a market to sell goods or services.

_________ practice tends to be seen as a creative industry, which includes advertising, distribution and selling.

a. Marketing myopia
b. Product naming
c. Customer acquisition management
d. Marketing

3. _________ in organizations and public policy is both the organizational process of creating and maintaining a plan; and the psychological process of thinking about the activities required to create a desired goal on some scale. As such, it is a fundamental property of intelligent behavior. This thought process is essential to the creation and refinement of a plan, or integration of it with other plans, that is, it combines forecasting of developments with the preparation of scenarios of how to react to them.

a. 180SearchAssistant
b. 6-3-5 Brainwriting
c. Power III
d. Planning

4. _________ is the realization of an application idea, model, design, specification, standard, algorithm an _________ is a realization of a technical specification or algorithm as a program, software component, or other computer system. Many _________s may exist for a given specification or standard.

a. ACNielsen
b. AMAX
c. ADTECH
d. Implementation

5. A _________ is a written document that details the necessary actions to achieve one or more marketing objectives. It can be for a product or service, a brand, or a product line. _________s cover between one and five years.

a. Prosumer
b. Marketing plan
c. Disruptive technology
d. Marketing strategy

6. Human beings are also considered to be _________ because they have the ability to change raw materials into valuable _________. The term Human _________ can also be defined as the skills, energies, talents, abilities and knowledge that are used for the production of goods or the rendering of services. While taking into account human beings as _________, the following things have to be kept in mind:

- The size of the population
- The capabilities of the individuals in that population

Many _________ cannot be consumed in their original form. They have to be processed in order to change them into more usable commodities.

a. Power III
b. 6-3-5 Brainwriting
c. Resources
d. 180SearchAssistant

7. A _________ is a brief statement of the purpose of a company, organization. It is ideally used to guide the actions of the organization.

_________s often contain the following:

- Purpose of the organization
- The organization's primary stakeholders: clients, stockholders, etc.
- Responsibilities of the organization towards these stockholders
- Products and services offered

Generally shorter _________s are more effective than longer ones.

In developing a _________:

- Encourage input as feasible from employees, volunteers, and other stakeholders
- Publicize it broadly

The _________ can be used to resolve differences between business stakeholders. Stakeholders include: employees including managers and executives, stockholders, board of directors, customers, suppliers, distributors, creditors, governments (local, state, federal, etc.), unions, competitors, NGO's, and the general public.

a. 6-3-5 Brainwriting
b. Mission statement
c. 180SearchAssistant
d. Power III

8. Competitiveness is a comparative concept of the ability and performance of a firm, sub-sector or country to sell and supply goods and/or services in a given market. Although widely used in economics and business management, the usefulness of the concept, particularly in the context of national competitiveness, is vigorously disputed by economists, such as Paul Krugman .

The term may also be applied to markets, where it is used to refer to the extent to which the market structure may be regarded as perfectly _________.

a. Free trade zone
b. Competitive
c. Geographical pricing
d. Customs union

9. _________ is, in very basic words, a position a firm occupies against its competitors.

According to Michael Porter, the three methods for creating a sustainable _________ are through:

1. Cost leadership - Cost advantage occurs when a firm delivers the same services as its competitors but at a lower cost;

2.

a. 180SearchAssistant
b. Power III
c. Competitive advantage
d. 6-3-5 Brainwriting

10.

Competitive advantage is, in very basic words, a position a firm occupies against its competitors. According to Michael Porter, the three methods for creating a _________ are through:

Cost leadership - Cost advantage occurs when a firm delivers the same services as its competitors but at a lower cost;

Differentiation - Differentiation advantage occurs when a firm delivers greater services for the same price of its competitors. They are collectively known as positional advantages because they denote the firm's position in its industry as a leader in either superior services or cost;

Focus (economics) - A focused approach requires the firm to concentrate on a narrow, exclusive competitive segment (market niche), hoping to achieve a local rather than industry wide competitive advantage. There are cost focus seekers, who aim to obtain a local cost advantage over competition and differentiation focuser, who are looking for a local difference.

a. 180SearchAssistant
b. Power III
c. Sustainable competitive advantage
d. 6-3-5 Brainwriting

11. _________ is a strategic planning method used to evaluate the Strengths, Weaknesses, Opportunities, and Threats involved in a project or in a business venture. It involves specifying the objective of the business venture or project and identifying the internal and external factors that are favorable and unfavorable to achieving that objective. The technique is credited to Albert Humphrey, who led a research project at Stanford University in the 1960s and 1970s using data from Fortune 500 companies.

a. Lead scoring
b. Product differentiation
c. Market environment
d. SWOT analysis

12. _________ is a marketing term, and involves evaluating the situation and trends in a particular company's market. _________ is often called the 'three c's', which refers to the three major elements that must be studied:

- Customers
- Costs
- Competition

The number of 'c's' is sometimes extended to four, five, or even six, with 'Collaboration', 'Company', and 'Competitive advantage'.

- Marketing mix
- SWOT analysis

.

a. Situation analysis
b. 180SearchAssistant
c. Power III
d. 6-3-5 Brainwriting

13. In economics ' business, specifically cost accounting, the _________ is the point at which cost or expenses and revenue are equal: there is no net loss or gain, and one has 'broken even'. A profit or a loss has not been made, although opportunity costs have been paid, and capital has received the risk-adjusted, expected return.

For example, if the business sells less than 200 tables each month, it will make a loss, if it sells more, it will be a profit.

a. Total revenue
b. Power III
c. Break-even point
d. 180SearchAssistant

14. A _________ is a subgroup of people or organizations sharing one or more characteristics that cause them to have similar product and/or service needs. A true _________ meets all of the following criteria: it is distinct from other segments (different segments have different needs), it is homogeneous within the segment (exhibits common needs); it responds similarly to a market stimulus, and it can be reached by a market intervention. The term is also used when consumers with identical product and/or service needs are divided up into groups so they can be charged different amounts.

a. Customer insight
b. Production orientation
c. Commercial planning
d. Market segment

15. In marketing, _________ has come to mean the process by which marketers try to create an image or identity in the minds of their target market for its product, brand, or organization. It is the 'relative competitive comparison' their product occupies in a given market as perceived by the target market.

Re-_________ involves changing the identity of a product, relative to the identity of competing products, in the collective minds of the target market.

a. Moratorium
b. Containerization
c. GE matrix
d. Positioning

16. In marketing and advertising, a _________ usually an advertising campaign, is aimed at appealing to. A _________ can be people of a certain age group, gender, marital status, etc. (ex: teenagers, females, single people, etc.)

a. National brand
b. Target audience
c. Brand Development Index
d. Targeted advertising

17. The _________ is generally accepted as the use and specification of the four p's describing the strategic position of a product in the marketplace. One version of the origins of the _________ starts in 1948 when James Culliton said that a marketing decision should be a result of something similar to a recipe. This version continued in 1953 when Neil Borden, in his American Marketing Association presidential address, took the recipe idea one step further and coined the term 'Marketing-Mix'.

a. 6-3-5 Brainwriting
b. 180SearchAssistant
c. Marketing mix
d. Power III

18. A personal and cultural _________ is a relative ethic _________, an assumption upon which implementation can be extrapolated. A _________ system is a set of consistent _________s and measures that is soo not true. A principle _________ is a foundation upon which other _________s and measures of integrity are based.

a. Perceptual maps
b. Package-on-Package
c. Supreme Court of the United States
d. Value

19. _________, or Value optimized pricing is a business strategy. It sets selling prices on the perceived value to the customer, rather than on the actual cost of the product, the market price, competitors prices, or the historical price.

The goal of _________ is to align price with value delivered.

a. Value-based pricing
b. Money back guarantee
c. Jobbing house
d. Service-profit chain

20. A _________ is a collection of symbols, experiences and associations connected with a product, a service, a person or any other artifact or entity.

_________s have become increasingly important components of culture and the economy, now being described as 'cultural accessories and personal philosophies'.

Some people distinguish the psychological aspect of a _________ from the experiential aspect.

a. Brand
b. Store brand
c. Brandable software
d. Brand equity

21. In economics, business, retail, and accounting, a _________ is the value of money that has been used up to produce something, and hence is not available for use anymore. In economics, a _________ is an alternative that is given up as a result of a decision. In business, the _________ may be one of acquisition, in which case the amount of money expended to acquire it is counted as _________.

a. Cost
b. Fixed costs
c. Variable cost
d. Transaction cost

22. _________ is the state or fact of exclusive rights and control over property, which may be an object, land/real estate, or some other kind of property (like government-granted monopolies collectively referred to as intellectual property.) It is embodied in an _________ right also referred to as title.

_________ is the key building block in the development of the capitalist socio-economic system.

a. ACNielsen
b. AMAX
c. Ownership
d. ADTECH

23. _________ in economics and business is the result of an exchange and from that trade we assign a numerical monetary value to a good, service or asset. If I trade 4 apples for an orange, the _________ of an orange is 4 - apples. Inversely, the _________ of an apple is 1/4 oranges.

a. Pricing
b. Discounts and allowances
c. Contribution margin-based pricing
d. Price

24. _________ is one of the four Ps of the marketing mix. The other three aspects are product, promotion, and place. It is also a key variable in microeconomic price allocation theory.

a. Competitor indexing
b. Pricing
c. Price
d. Relationship based pricing

25. In business and engineering, new _________ is the term used to describe the complete process of bringing a new product or service to market. There are two parallel paths involved in the Nproduct development process: one involves the idea generation, product design, and detail engineering; the other involves market research and marketing analysis. Companies typically see new _________ as the first stage in generating and commercializing new products within the overall strategic process of product life cycle management used to maintain or grow their market share.

a. Specification tree
b. New product screening
c. Product development
d. New product development

26. A _________ or logistics network is the system of organizations, people, technology, activities, information and resources involved in moving a product or service from supplier to customer. _________ activities transform natural resources, raw materials and components into a finished product that is delivered to the end customer. In sophisticated _________ systems, used products may re-enter the _________ at any point where residual value is recyclable.

a. Supply chain network
b. Purchasing
c. Demand chain management
d. Supply chain

27. _________ is a list for goods and materials held available in stock by a business. It is also used for a list of the contents of a household and for a list for testamentary purposes of the possessions of someone who has died. In accounting _________ is considered an asset.

a. ADTECH
b. Ending Inventory
c. Inventory
d. ACNielsen

28. _________ , according to The American Marketing Association, is 'a planning process designed to assure that all brand contacts received by a customer or prospect for a product, service, or organization are relevant to that person and consistent over time.' (Marketing Power Dictionary)

_________ is a term used to describe a holistic approach to marketing. It aims to ensure consistency of message and the complementary use of media. The concept includes online and offline marketing channels.

a. ACNielsen
b. ADTECH
c. AMAX
d. Integrated marketing communications

29. There are many important decisions about product and service development and marketing. In the process of product development and marketing we should focus on strategic decisions about product attributes, product branding, product packaging, product labeling and product support services. But product strategy also calls for building a _________.

a. Pinstorm
b. Macromarketing
c. Technology acceptance model
d. Product line

30. _________ involves disseminating information about a product, product line, brand, or company. It is one of the four key aspects of the marketing mix. (The other three elements are product marketing, pricing, and distribution). P>_________ is generally sub-divided into two parts:

- Above the line _________: Promotion in the media (e.g. TV, radio, newspapers, Internet and Mobile Phones) in which the advertiser pays an advertising agency to place the ad
- Below the line _________: All other _________. Much of this is intended to be subtle enough for the consumer to be unaware that _________ is taking place. E.g. sponsorship, product placement, endorsements, sales _________, merchandising, direct mail, personal selling, public relations, trade shows

a. Davie Brown Index
b. Cashmere Agency
c. Bottling lines
d. Promotion

31. _________ is a broad label that refers to any individuals or households that use goods and services generated within the economy. The concept of a _________ is used in different contexts, so that the usage and significance of the term may vary.

A _________ is a person who uses any product or service.

a. 6-3-5 Brainwriting
b. 180SearchAssistant
c. Power III
d. Consumer

32. _________ is the study of when, why, how, where and what people do or do not buy products. It blends elements from psychology, sociology,social psychology, anthropology and economics. It attempts to understand the buyer decision making process, both individually and in groups. It studies characteristics of individual consumers such as demographics and behavioural variables in an attempt to understand people's wants. It also tries to assess influences on the consumer from groups such as family, friends, reference groups, and society in general.

a. Consumer confidence
b. Communal marketing
c. Multidimensional scaling
d. Consumer behavior

33. _________ refers to messages and related media used to communicate with a market. Those who practice advertising, branding, direct marketing, graphic design, marketing, packaging, promotion, publicity, sponsorship, public relations, sales, sales promotion and online marketing are termed marketing communicators, _________ managers, or more briefly as marcom managers.

a. Sales promotion
b. Marketing communication
c. Merchandising
d. Merchandise

34. _________ is systematic determination of merit, worth, and significance of something or someone using criteria against a set of standards. _________ often is used to characterize and appraise subjects of interest in a wide range of human enterprises, including the arts, criminal justice, foundations and non-profit organizations, government, health care, and other human services.

Depending on the topic of interest, there are professional groups which look to the quality and rigor of the _________ process.

a. ACNielsen
b. ADTECH
c. AMAX
d. Evaluation

35. _________ is a form of communication that typically attempts to persuade potential customers to purchase or to consume more of a particular brand of product or service. 'While now central to the contemporary global economy and the reproduction of global production networks, it is only quite recently that _________ has been more than a marginal influence on patterns of sales and production. The formation of modern _________ was intimately bound up with the emergence of new forms of monopoly capitalism around the end of the 19th and beginning of the 20th century as one element in corporate strategies to create, organize and where possible control markets, especially for mass produced consumer goods.

a. ADTECH
b. AMAX
c. ACNielsen
d. Advertising

36. An _________ is a series of advertisement messages that share a single idea and theme which make up an integrated marketing communication (IMC.) _________s appear in different media across a specific time frame.

The critical part of making an _________ is determining a campaign theme, as it sets the tone for the individual advertisements and other forms of marketing communications that will be used.

a. ADTECH
b. AMAX
c. ACNielsen
d. Advertising campaign

37. _________ is one of the four growth strategies of the Product-Market Growth Matrix defined by Ansoff. _________ occurs when a company enters/penetrates a market with current products. The best way to achieve this is by gaining competitors' customers (part of their market share.)

a. Pasar pagi
b. Horizontal market
c. Marketization
d. Market penetration

38. A _________ is a plan of action designed to achieve a particular goal.

_________ is different from tactics. In military terms, tactics is concerned with the conduct of an engagement while _________ is concerned with how different engagements are linked.

a. 180SearchAssistant
b. 6-3-5 Brainwriting
c. Power III
d. Strategy

39. A _________ strategy targets non-buying customers in currently targeted segments. It also targets new customers in new segments. (Winer)

A marketing manager has to think about the following questions before implementing a _________ strategy: Is it profitable? Will it require the introduction of new or modified products? Is the customer and channel well enough researched and understood?

The marketing manager uses these four groups to give more focus to the market segment decision: existing customers, competitor customers, non-buying in current segments, new segments.

a. Kano model
b. Market development
c. Commercial planning
d. Perceptual mapping

40. In economics, _________ is the desire to own something and the ability to pay for it. The term _________ signifies the ability or the willingness to buy a particular commodity at a given point of time .

a. Market system
b. Market dominance
c. Discretionary spending
d. Demand

41. In economics, the _________ can be defined as the graph depicting the relationship between the price of a certain commodity, and the amount of it that consumers are willing and able to purchase at that given price. It is a graphic representation of a demand schedule The _________ for all consumers together follows from the _________ of every individual consumer: the individual demands at each price are added together.

_________s are used to estimate behaviors in competitive markets, and are often combined with supply curves to estimate the equilibrium price (the price at which sellers together are willing to sell the same amount as buyers together are willing to buy, also known as market clearing price) and the equilibrium quantity (the amount of that good or service that will be produced and bought without surplus/excess supply or shortage/excess demand) of that market.

a. 6-3-5 Brainwriting
b. Power III
c. 180SearchAssistant
d. Demand curve

42. _________ is the provision of service to customers before, during and after a purchase.

According to Turban et al., '_________ is a series of activities designed to enhance the level of customer satisfaction - that is, the feeling that a product or service has met the customer expectation.'

Its importance varies by product, industry and customer.

a. Customer experience
b. Facing
c. COPC Inc.
d. Customer service

43. _________ is an advertisement in which a particular product specifically mentions a competitor by name for the express purpose of showing why the competitor is inferior to the product naming it.

This should not be confused with parody advertisements, where a fictional product is being advertised for the purpose of poking fun at the particular advertisement, nor should it be confused with the use of a coined brand name for the purpose of comparing the product without actually naming an actual competitor. ('Wikipedia tastes better and is less filling than the Encyclopedia Galactica.')

In the 1980s, during what has been referred to as the cola wars, soft-drink manufacturer Pepsi ran a series of advertisements where people, caught on hidden camera, in a blind taste test, chose Pepsi over rival Coca-Cola.

a. GL-70
b. Cost per conversion
c. Heavy-up
d. Comparative advertising

44. The _________ is a chart that had been created by Bruce Henderson for the Boston Consulting Group in 1970 to help corporations with analyzing their business units or product lines. This helps the company allocate resources and is used as an analytical tool in brand marketing, product management, strategic management, and portfolio analysis.

a. Sports Marketing Group
b. AStore
c. Sampling
d. BCG matrix

45. _________, in strategic management and marketing, is the percentage or proportion of the total available market or market segment that is being serviced by a company. It can be expressed as a company's sales revenue (from that market) divided by the total sales revenue available in that market. It can also be expressed as a company's unit sales volume (in a market) divided by the total volume of units sold in that market.

a. Demand generation
b. Cyberdoc
c. Customer relationship management
d. Market share

46. In business, a _________ is a product or a business unit that generates unusually high profit margins: so high that it is responsible for a large amount of a company's operating profit. This profit far exceeds the amount necessary to maintain the _________ business, and the excess is used by the business for other purposes.

A firm is said to be acting as a _________ when its earnings per share (EPS) is equal to its dividends per share (DPS), or in other words, when a firm pays out 100% of its free cash flow (FCF) to its shareholders as dividends at the end of each accounting term.

a. Goal setting
b. Crisis management
c. Corporate transparency
d. Cash cow

1. _________ is a branch of philosophy which seeks to address questions about morality, such as how a moral outcome can be achieved in a specific situation (applied _________), how moral values should be determined (normative _________), what moral values people actually abide by (descriptive _________), what the fundamental semantic, ontological, and epistemic nature of _________ or morality is (meta-_________), and how moral capacity or moral agency develops and what its nature is (moral psychology.)

Socrates was one of the first Greek philosophers to encourage both scholars and the common citizen to turn their attention from the outside world to the condition of man. In this view, Knowledge having a bearing on human life was placed highest, all other knowledge being secondary.

a. Ethics
b. ADTECH
c. AMAX
d. ACNielsen

2. _________ is a form of communication that typically attempts to persuade potential customers to purchase or to consume more of a particular brand of product or service. 'While now central to the contemporary global economy and the reproduction of global production networks, it is only quite recently that _________ has been more than a marginal influence on patterns of sales and production. The formation of modern _________ was intimately bound up with the emergence of new forms of monopoly capitalism around the end of the 19th and beginning of the 20th century as one element in corporate strategies to create, organize and where possible control markets, especially for mass produced consumer goods.

a. AMAX
b. ADTECH
c. ACNielsen
d. Advertising

3. _________ is a form of applied ethics that examines ethical principles and moral or ethical problems that arise in a business environment. It applies to all aspects of business conduct and is relevant to the conduct of individuals and business organizations as a whole. Applied ethics is a field of ethics that deals with ethical questions in many fields such as medical, technical, legal and _________.

a. 6-3-5 Brainwriting
b. Power III
c. 180SearchAssistant
d. Business ethics

4. _________ is defined by the American _________ Association as the activity, set of institutions, and processes for creating, communicating, delivering, and exchanging offerings that have value for customers, clients, partners, and society at large. The term developed from the original meaning which referred literally to going to market, as in shopping, or going to a market to sell goods or services.

_________ practice tends to be seen as a creative industry, which includes advertising, distribution and selling.

a. Marketing
b. Marketing myopia
c. Customer acquisition management
d. Product naming

5. The _________ is a marketing term and refers to all of the forces outside of marketing that affect marketing management's ability to build and maintain successful relationships with target customers. The _________ consists of both the macroenvironment and the microenvironment.

The microenvironment refers to the forces that are close to the company and affect its ability to serve its customers.

a. Psychographic
b. Customer franchise
c. Business-to-consumer
d. Market environment

6. _________ is the area of applied ethics which deals with the moral principles behind the operation and regulation of marketing. Some areas of _________ overlap with media ethics.

Possible frameworks:

- Value-oriented framework, analyzing ethical problems on the basis of the values which they infringe (e.g. honesty, autonomy, privacy, transparency.) An example of such an approach is the AMA Statement of Ethics.
- Stakeholder-oriented framework, analysing ethical problems on the basis of whom they affect (e.g. consumers, competitors, society as a whole.)
- Process-oriented framework, analysing ethical problems in terms of the categories used by marketing specialists (e.g. research, price, promotion, placement.)

None of these frameworks allows, by itself, a convenient and complete categorization of the great variety of issues in _________.

Contrary to popular impressions, not all marketing is adversarial, and not all marketing is stacked in favour of the marketer.

a. 6-3-5 Brainwriting
b. Power III
c. 180SearchAssistant
d. Marketing ethics

7. The _________ is a professional association for marketers. As of 2008 it had approximately 40,000 members. There are collegiate chapters on 250 campuses.

a. American Marketing Association
b. ADTECH
c. ACNielsen
d. AMAX

8. _________ also known as corporate responsibility, corporate citizenship, responsible business, sustainable responsible business and corporate social performance' is a form of corporate self-regulation integrated into a business model. Ideally, _________ policy would function as a built-in, self-regulating mechanism whereby business would monitor and ensure their adherence to law, ethical standards, and international norms. Business would embrace responsibility for the impact of their activities on the environment, consumers, employees, communities, stakeholders and all other members of the public sphere.

a. 6-3-5 Brainwriting
b. Corporate social responsibility
c. Power III
d. 180SearchAssistant

9. _________ is a broad label that refers to any individuals or households that use goods and services generated within the economy. The concept of a _________ is used in different contexts, so that the usage and significance of the term may vary.

A _________ is a person who uses any product or service.

a. Consumer
b. Power III
c. 6-3-5 Brainwriting
d. 180SearchAssistant

10. _________ is the study of when, why, how, where and what people do or do not buy products. It blends elements from psychology, sociology,social psychology, anthropology and economics. It attempts to understand the buyer decision making process, both individually and in groups. It studies characteristics of individual consumers such as demographics and behavioural variables in an attempt to understand people's wants. It also tries to assess influences on the consumer from groups such as family, friends, reference groups, and society in general.

a. Consumer behavior
b. Consumer confidence
c. Multidimensional scaling
d. Communal marketing

11. _________ in organizations and public policy is both the organizational process of creating and maintaining a plan; and the psychological process of thinking about the activities required to create a desired goal on some scale. As such, it is a fundamental property of intelligent behavior. This thought process is essential to the creation and refinement of a plan, or integration of it with other plans, that is, it combines forecasting of developments with the preparation of scenarios of how to react to them.

a. Power III
b. 6-3-5 Brainwriting
c. 180SearchAssistant
d. Planning

12. Radio-frequency identification (_________) is the use of an object (typically referred to as an _________ tag) applied to or incorporated into a product, animal, or person for the purpose of identification and tracking using radio waves. Some tags can be read from several meters away and beyond the line of sight of the reader.

Most _________ tags contain at least two parts.

a. 180SearchAssistant
b. Power III
c. 6-3-5 Brainwriting
d. RFID

13. _________ involves disseminating information about a product, product line, brand, or company. It is one of the four key aspects of the marketing mix. (The other three elements are product marketing, pricing, and distribution). P>_________ is generally sub-divided into two parts:

- Above the line _________: Promotion in the media (e.g. TV, radio, newspapers, Internet and Mobile Phones) in which the advertiser pays an advertising agency to place the ad
- Below the line _________: All other _________. Much of this is intended to be subtle enough for the consumer to be unaware that _________ is taking place. E.g. sponsorship, product placement, endorsements, sales _________, merchandising, direct mail, personal selling, public relations, trade shows

a. Bottling lines
b. Cashmere Agency
c. Davie Brown Index
d. Promotion

14. _________ is one of the four aspects of promotional mix. (The other three parts of the promotional mix are advertising, personal selling, and publicity/public relations.) Media and non-media marketing communication are employed for a pre-determined, limited time to increase consumer demand, stimulate market demand or improve product availability.

a. Marketing communication
b. Merchandise
c. Sales promotion
d. New Media Strategies

15. _________ is the realization of an application idea, model, design, specification, standard, algorithm an _________ is a realization of a technical specification or algorithm as a program, software component, or other computer system. Many _________s may exist for a given specification or standard.

a. ADTECH
b. AMAX
c. Implementation
d. ACNielsen

16. A _________ is a process that can allow an organization to concentrate its limited resources on the greatest opportunities to increase sales and achieve a sustainable competitive advantage. A _________ should be centered around the key concept that customer satisfaction is the main goal.

A _________ is most effective when it is an integral component of corporate strategy, defining how the organization will successfully engage customers, prospects, and competitors in the market arena.

a. Marketing strategy
b. Psychographic
c. Cyberdoc
d. Societal marketing

17. A _________ is a plan of action designed to achieve a particular goal.

_________ is different from tactics. In military terms, tactics is concerned with the conduct of an engagement while _________ is concerned with how different engagements are linked.

a. 180SearchAssistant
b. 6-3-5 Brainwriting
c. Power III
d. Strategy

18. _________ is a sub-discipline and type of marketing. There are two main definitional characteristics which distinguish it from other types of marketing. The first is that it attempts to send its messages directly to consumers, without the use of intervening media.

a. Direct Marketing Associations
b. Direct Marketing
c. Database marketing
d. Power III

19. _________ are national trade organizations that seek to advance all forms of direct marketing.

23 direct marketing trade associations from five continents established an International Federation of _________. Founded in 1989, the IFDirect Marketing Associations was established to develop firm lines of communications between direct marketers around the world, and is dedicated to improving the practice and communicating the value of direct marketing; and to promoting the highest standards for ethical conduct and effective self-regulation of the direct marketing community.

a. Power III
b. Direct marketing
c. Direct Marketing Associations
d. Database marketing

1. Competitiveness is a comparative concept of the ability and performance of a firm, sub-sector or country to sell and supply goods and/or services in a given market. Although widely used in economics and business management, the usefulness of the concept, particularly in the context of national competitiveness, is vigorously disputed by economists, such as Paul Krugman .

The term may also be applied to markets, where it is used to refer to the extent to which the market structure may be regarded as perfectly _________.

a. Customs union
b. Competitive
c. Free trade zone
d. Geographical pricing

2. _________ is a list for goods and materials held available in stock by a business. It is also used for a list of the contents of a household and for a list for testamentary purposes of the possessions of someone who has died. In accounting _________ is considered an asset.

a. ADTECH
b. Ending Inventory
c. ACNielsen
d. Inventory

3. _________ is an inventory strategy implemented to improve the return on investment of a business by reducing in-process inventory and its associated carrying costs. In order to achieve JIT the process must have signals of what is going on elsewhere within the process. This means that the process is often driven by a series of signals, which can be Kanban , that tell production processes when to make the next part.

a. Personalization
b. Just-in-time
c. Promotion
d. Clutter

4. _________ is difficult to define. For example, in 1952, Alfred Kroeber and Clyde Kluckhohn compiled a list of 164 definitions of '_________' in _________: A Critical Review of Concepts and Definitions. However, the word '_________' is most commonly used in three basic senses:

- excellence of taste in the fine arts and humanities
- an integrated pattern of human knowledge, belief, and behavior that depends upon the capacity for symbolic thought and social learning
- the set of shared attitudes, values, goals, and practices that characterizes an institution, organization or group.

When the concept first emerged in eighteenth- and nineteenth-century Europe, it connoted a process of cultivation or improvement, as in agriculture or horticulture. In the nineteenth century, it came to refer first to the betterment or refinement of the individual, especially through education, and then to the fulfillment of national aspirations or ideals.

a. AStore
b. African Americans
c. Albert Einstein
d. Culture

5. _________ is a term used to describe a person who was born during the demographic Post-World War II baby boom. Many analysts now believe that two distinct cultural generations were born during this baby boom; the older generation is often called the Baby Boom Generation and the younger generation is often called Generation Jones. The term '_________' is sometimes used in a cultural context, and sometimes used to describe someone who was born during the post-WWII baby boom.

a. Greatest Generation
b. Generation X
c. AStore
d. Baby Boomer

6. The United States _________ is the government agency that is responsible for the United States Census. It also gathers other national demographic and economic data.

a. 180SearchAssistant
b. 6-3-5 Brainwriting
c. Census Bureau
d. Power III

7. _________ or _________ data refers to selected population characteristics as used in government, marketing or opinion research, or the _________ profiles used in such research. Note the distinction from the term 'demography' Commonly-used _________ include race, age, income, disabilities, mobility (in terms of travel time to work or number of vehicles available), educational attainment, home ownership, employment status, and even location.

a. Demographic
b. AStore
c. Albert Einstein
d. African Americans

8. _________ is a cohort which consists of those people born after the Generation X cohort. Its name is controversial and is synonymous with several alternative names including The Net Generation, Millennials, Echo Boomers, and iGeneration. _________ consists primarily of the offspring of the Generation Jones and Baby Boomers cohorts.

a. Greatest Generation
b. AStore
c. Generation Y
d. Generation X

9. _________ is a term used to identify people born after the post-World War II increase in birth rates (the baby boom) The term has been used in demography, the social sciences, and marketing, though it is most often used in popular culture.

In the U.S. _________ was originally referred to as the 'baby bust' generation because of the drop in the birth rate following the baby boom.

In the UK the term was first used in a 1964 study of British youth by Jane Deverson.

a. Generation X
b. Greatest Generation
c. AStore
d. Generation Y

10. _________ is one of the four growth strategies of the Product-Market Growth Matrix defined by Ansoff. _________ occurs when a company enters/penetrates a market with current products. The best way to achieve this is by gaining competitors' customers (part of their market share.)

a. Horizontal market
b. Pasar pagi
c. Market penetration
d. Marketization

11. _________ is the practice of selling a product or service at a very low price, intending to drive competitors out of the market, or create barriers to entry for potential new competitors. If competitors or potential competitors cannot sustain equal or lower prices without losing money, they go out of business or choose not to enter the business. The predatory merchant then has fewer competitors or is even a de facto monopoly, and can then raise prices above what the market would otherwise bear.

a. Predatory pricing
b. 180SearchAssistant
c. Power III
d. List price

12. According to the American Marketing Association, _________ is the marketing of products that are presumed to be environmentally safe. Thus _________ incorporates a broad range of activities, including product modification, changes to the production process, packaging changes, as well as modifying advertising. Yet defining _________ is not a simple task where several meanings intersect and contradict each other; an example of this will be the existence of varying social, environmental and retail definitions attached to this term.

a. Value proposition
b. Commercialization
c. Customer Interaction Tracker
d. Green marketing

13. _________ is defined by the American _________ Association as the activity, set of institutions, and processes for creating, communicating, delivering, and exchanging offerings that have value for customers, clients, partners, and society at large. The term developed from the original meaning which referred literally to going to market, as in shopping, or going to a market to sell goods or services.

_________ practice tends to be seen as a creative industry, which includes advertising, distribution and selling.

a. Marketing myopia
b. Product naming
c. Customer acquisition management
d. Marketing

14. _________ is a broad label that refers to any individuals or households that use goods and services generated within the economy. The concept of a _________ is used in different contexts, so that the usage and significance of the term may vary.

A _________ is a person who uses any product or service.

a. 180SearchAssistant
b. Power III
c. 6-3-5 Brainwriting
d. Consumer

15. _________ is the ability of an individual or group to seclude themselves or information about themselves and thereby reveal themselves selectively. The boundaries and content of what is considered private differ among cultures and individuals, but share basic common themes. _________ is sometimes related to anonymity, the wish to remain unnoticed or unidentified in the public realm.

a. 180SearchAssistant
b. 6-3-5 Brainwriting
c. Privacy
d. Power III

16. In economics, _________ is the desire to own something and the ability to pay for it. The term _________ signifies the ability or the willingness to buy a particular commodity at a given point of time .

.

a. Market dominance
b. Demand
c. Market system
d. Discretionary spending

17. In economics, the _________ can be defined as the graph depicting the relationship between the price of a certain commodity, and the amount of it that consumers are willing and able to purchase at that given price. It is a graphic representation of a demand schedule The _________ for all consumers together follows from the _________ of every individual consumer: the individual demands at each price are added together.

_________s are used to estimate behaviors in competitive markets, and are often combined with supply curves to estimate the equilibrium price (the price at which sellers together are willing to sell the same amount as buyers together are willing to buy, also known as market clearing price) and the equilibrium quantity (the amount of that good or service that will be produced and bought without surplus/excess supply or shortage/excess demand) of that market.

a. 180SearchAssistant
b. 6-3-5 Brainwriting
c. Power III
d. Demand curve

18. _________ is one of the four Ps of the marketing mix. The other three aspects are product, promotion, and place. It is also a key variable in microeconomic price allocation theory.

a. Relationship based pricing
b. Price
c. Competitor indexing
d. Pricing

19. _________s is the social science that studies the production, distribution, and consumption of goods and services. The term _________s comes from the Ancient Greek oá¼°κονομÎ¯α from oá¼¶κος (oikos, 'house') + νÏŒμος (nomos, 'custom' or 'law'), hence 'rules of the house(hold)'. Current _________ models developed out of the broader field of political economy in the late 19th century, owing to a desire to use an empirical approach more akin to the physical sciences.

a. Industrial organization
b. ADTECH
c. ACNielsen
d. Economic

20. In economics, _________ is a rise in the general level of prices of goods and services in an economy over a period of time. The term '_________' once referred to increases in the money supply (monetary _________); however, economic debates about the relationship between money supply and price levels have led to its primary use today in describing price _________. Inflation can also be described as a decline in the real value of money--a loss of purchasing power in the medium of exchange which is also the monetary unit of account.

a. Inflation
b. Industrial organization
c. ADTECH
d. ACNielsen

21. _________ is a fee paid on borrowed assets. It is the price paid for the use of borrowed money , or, money earned by deposited funds . Assets that are sometimes lent with _________ include money, shares, consumer goods through hire purchase, major assets such as aircraft, and even entire factories in finance lease arrangements.

a. ADTECH
b. AMAX
c. ACNielsen
d. Interest

22. _________ in organizations and public policy is both the organizational process of creating and maintaining a plan; and the psychological process of thinking about the activities required to create a desired goal on some scale. As such, it is a fundamental property of intelligent behavior. This thought process is essential to the creation and refinement of a plan, or integration of it with other plans, that is, it combines forecasting of developments with the preparation of scenarios of how to react to them.

a. Power III
b. 180SearchAssistant
c. Planning
d. 6-3-5 Brainwriting

23. _________ is a strategic planning method used to evaluate the Strengths, Weaknesses, Opportunities, and Threats involved in a project or in a business venture. It involves specifying the objective of the business venture or project and identifying the internal and external factors that are favorable and unfavorable to achieving that objective. The technique is credited to Albert Humphrey, who led a research project at Stanford University in the 1960s and 1970s using data from Fortune 500 companies.

a. Lead scoring
b. Market environment
c. SWOT analysis
d. Product differentiation

24. The _________ is generally accepted as the use and specification of the four p's describing the strategic position of a product in the marketplace. One version of the origins of the _________ starts in 1948 when James Culliton said that a marketing decision should be a result of something similar to a recipe. This version continued in 1953 when Neil Borden, in his American Marketing Association presidential address, took the recipe idea one step further and coined the term 'Marketing-Mix'.

a. Marketing mix
b. Power III
c. 6-3-5 Brainwriting
d. 180SearchAssistant

25. _________ is systematic determination of merit, worth, and significance of something or someone using criteria against a set of standards. _________ often is used to characterize and appraise subjects of interest in a wide range of human enterprises, including the arts, criminal justice, foundations and non-profit organizations, government, health care, and other human services.

Depending on the topic of interest, there are professional groups which look to the quality and rigor of the _________ process.

a. AMAX
b. ADTECH
c. ACNielsen
d. Evaluation

26. _________ is a form of communication that typically attempts to persuade potential customers to purchase or to consume more of a particular brand of product or service. 'While now central to the contemporary global economy and the reproduction of global production networks, it is only quite recently that _________ has been more than a marginal influence on patterns of sales and production. The formation of modern _________ was intimately bound up with the emergence of new forms of monopoly capitalism around the end of the 19th and beginning of the 20th century as one element in corporate strategies to create, organize and where possible control markets, especially for mass produced consumer goods.

a. Advertising
b. ACNielsen
c. AMAX
d. ADTECH

27. An _________ is a series of advertisement messages that share a single idea and theme which make up an integrated marketing communication (IMC.) _________s appear in different media across a specific time frame.

The critical part of making an _________ is determining a campaign theme, as it sets the tone for the individual advertisements and other forms of marketing communications that will be used.

a. AMAX
b. ACNielsen
c. ADTECH
d. Advertising campaign

1. _________ is a broad label that refers to any individuals or households that use goods and services generated within the economy. The concept of a _________ is used in different contexts, so that the usage and significance of the term may vary.

A _________ is a person who uses any product or service.

a. 6-3-5 Brainwriting
b. Power III
c. 180SearchAssistant
d. Consumer

2. _________ is the study of when, why, how, where and what people do or do not buy products. It blends elements from psychology, sociology,social psychology, anthropology and economics. It attempts to understand the buyer decision making process, both individually and in groups. It studies characteristics of individual consumers such as demographics and behavioural variables in an attempt to understand people's wants. It also tries to assess influences on the consumer from groups such as family, friends, reference groups, and society in general.

a. Consumer confidence
b. Communal marketing
c. Consumer behavior
d. Multidimensional scaling

3. An _________ is an unplanned or otherwise spontaneous purchase. One who tends to make such purchases is referred to as an impulse purchaser or impulse buyer.

Marketers and retailers tend to exploit these impulses which are tied to the basic want for instant gratification.

a. ADTECH
b. Impulse purchase
c. ACNielsen
d. AMAX

4. _________ can be regarded as an outcome of mental processes (cognitive process) leading to the selection of a course of action among several alternatives. Every _________ process produces a final choice. The output can be an action or an opinion of choice.

a. 180SearchAssistant
b. Power III
c. Decision making
d. 6-3-5 Brainwriting

5. _________ is an American magazine published monthly by Consumers Union. It publishes reviews and comparisons of consumer products and services based on reporting and results from its in-house testing laboratory. It also publishes cleaning and general buying guides.

a. Power III
b. Consumer Reports
c. Magalog
d. Crossing the Chasm

6. In economics, an externality or spillover of an economic transaction is an impact on a party that is not directly involved in the transaction. In such a case, prices do not reflect the full costs or benefits in production or consumption of a product or service. A positive impact is called an _________ benefit, while a negative impact is called an _________ cost.

a. ADTECH
b. ACNielsen
c. AMAX
d. External

7. In economics, business, retail, and accounting, a _________ is the value of money that has been used up to produce something, and hence is not available for use anymore. In economics, a _________ is an alternative that is given up as a result of a decision. In business, the _________ may be one of acquisition, in which case the amount of money expended to acquire it is counted as _________.

a. Variable cost
b. Transaction cost
c. Fixed costs
d. Cost

8. _________ is a concept that denotes the precise probability of specific eventualities. Technically, the notion of _________ is independent from the notion of value and, as such, eventualities may have both beneficial and adverse consequences. However, in general usage the convention is to focus only on potential negative impact to some characteristic of value that may arise from a future event.

a. 180SearchAssistant
b. Power III
c. 6-3-5 Brainwriting
d. Risk

9. _________ is the examining of goods or services from retailers with the intent to purchase at that time. _________ is an activity of selection and/or purchase. In some contexts it is considered a leisure activity as well as an economic one.

a. Shopping
b. Discount store
c. Hawkers
d. Khodebshchik

10. _________ is an advertisement in which a particular product specifically mentions a competitor by name for the express purpose of showing why the competitor is inferior to the product naming it.

This should not be confused with parody advertisements, where a fictional product is being advertised for the purpose of poking fun at the particular advertisement, nor should it be confused with the use of a coined brand name for the purpose of comparing the product without actually naming an actual competitor. ('Wikipedia tastes better and is less filling than the Encyclopedia Galactica.')

In the 1980s, during what has been referred to as the cola wars, soft-drink manufacturer Pepsi ran a series of advertisements where people, caught on hidden camera, in a blind taste test, chose Pepsi over rival Coca-Cola.

a. Cost per conversion
b. Comparative advertising
c. GL-70
d. Heavy-up

11. In algebra, a _________ is a function depending on n that associates a scalar, det(A), to an n×n square matrix A. The fundamental geometric meaning of a _________ is a scale factor for measure when A is regarded as a linear transformation. _________s are important both in calculus, where they enter the substitution rule for several variables, and in multilinear algebra.

For a fixed nonnegative integer n, there is a unique _________ function for the n×n matrices over any commutative ring R. In particular, this function exists when R is the field of real or complex numbers.

a. Determinant
b. Motion Picture Association of America's film-rating system
c. Package-on-Package
d. Black Friday

12. _________ is systematic determination of merit, worth, and significance of something or someone using criteria against a set of standards. _________ often is used to characterize and appraise subjects of interest in a wide range of human enterprises, including the arts, criminal justice, foundations and non-profit organizations, government, health care, and other human services.

Depending on the topic of interest, there are professional groups which look to the quality and rigor of the _________ process.

a. ADTECH
b. ACNielsen
c. Evaluation
d. AMAX

13. _________ is a form of communication that typically attempts to persuade potential customers to purchase or to consume more of a particular brand of product or service. 'While now central to the contemporary global economy and the reproduction of global production networks, it is only quite recently that _________ has been more than a marginal influence on patterns of sales and production. The formation of modern _________ was intimately bound up with the emergence of new forms of monopoly capitalism around the end of the 19th and beginning of the 20th century as one element in corporate strategies to create, organize and where possible control markets, especially for mass produced consumer goods.

a. ACNielsen
b. ADTECH
c. AMAX
d. Advertising

14. An _________ is a series of advertisement messages that share a single idea and theme which make up an integrated marketing communication (IMC.) _________s appear in different media across a specific time frame.

The critical part of making an _________ is determining a campaign theme, as it sets the tone for the individual advertisements and other forms of marketing communications that will be used.

a. ACNielsen
b. Advertising campaign
c. AMAX
d. ADTECH

15. A set of _________ is the verbal equivalent of a graphical decision tree, which specifies class membership based on a hierarchical sequence of (contingent) decisions. Each rule in a set of _________ therefore generally takes the form of a Horn clause wherein class membership is implied by a conjunction of contingent observations.

IF $condition_1$ AND $condition_2$ AND ...

a. 6-3-5 Brainwriting
b. Decision rules
c. 180SearchAssistant
d. Power III

16. A _________ is a collection of symbols, experiences and associations connected with a product, a service, a person or any other artifact or entity.

_________s have become increasingly important components of culture and the economy, now being described as 'cultural accessories and personal philosophies'.

Some people distinguish the psychological aspect of a _________ from the experiential aspect.

a. Brandable software
b. Store brand
c. Brand equity
d. Brand

17. _________, a business term, is a measure of how products and services supplied by a company meet or surpass customer expectation. It is seen as a key performance indicator within business and is part of the four perspectives of a Balanced Scorecard.

In a competitive marketplace where businesses compete for customers, _________ is seen as a key differentiator and increasingly has become a key element of business strategy.

a. Customer satisfaction
b. Psychological pricing
c. Customer base
d. Supplier diversity

18. _________ in economics and business is the result of an exchange and from that trade we assign a numerical monetary value to a good, service or asset. If I trade 4 apples for an orange, the _________ of an orange is 4 - apples. Inversely, the _________ of an apple is 1/4 oranges.

a. Price
b. Discounts and allowances
c. Contribution margin-based pricing
d. Pricing

19. In business and engineering, new _________ is the term used to describe the complete process of bringing a new product or service to market. There are two parallel paths involved in the Nproduct development process: one involves the idea generation, product design, and detail engineering; the other involves market research and marketing analysis. Companies typically see new _________ as the first stage in generating and commercializing new products within the overall strategic process of product life cycle management used to maintain or grow their market share.

a. Product development
b. New product screening
c. Specification tree
d. New product development

20. _________ is a rivalry between individuals, groups, nations for territory, a niche, or allocation of resources. It arises whenever two or more parties strive for a goal which cannot be shared. _________ occurs naturally between living organisms which co-exist in the same environment.

a. Competition
b. Non-price competition
c. Price fixing
d. Price competition

21. _________ is one of the four Ps of the marketing mix. The other three aspects are product, promotion, and place. It is also a key variable in microeconomic price allocation theory.

a. Competitor indexing
b. Price
c. Pricing
d. Relationship based pricing

22. In marketing, _________ has come to mean the process by which marketers try to create an image or identity in the minds of their target market for its product, brand, or organization. It is the 'relative competitive comparison' their product occupies in a given market as perceived by the target market.

Re-_________ involves changing the identity of a product, relative to the identity of competing products, in the collective minds of the target market.

a. Moratorium
b. Containerization
c. Positioning
d. GE matrix

23. _________ is a reference to the passing of information from person to person. Originally the term referred specifically to oral communication (literally words from the mouth), but now includes any type of human communication, such as face to face, telephone, email, and text messaging.

Word-of-mouth marketing, which encompasses a variety of subcategories, including buzz, blog, viral, grassroots, cause influencers and social media marketing, as well as ambassador programs, work with consumer-generated media and more, can be highly valued by product marketers.

a. Marketing communication
b. New Media Strategies
c. Merchandise
d. Word of mouth

24. An _________ is a situation that will often involve an apparent conflict between moral imperatives, in which to obey one would result in transgressing another. This is also called an ethical paradox since in moral philosophy, paradox plays a central role in ethics debates. For instance, an ethical admonition to 'love thy neighbour as thy self' is not always just in contrast with, but sometimes in contradiction to an armed neighbour actively trying to kill you: if he or she succeeds, you will not be able to love him or her.

a. ADTECH
b. ACNielsen
c. AMAX
d. Ethical dilemma

25. In economics, _________ is the desire to own something and the ability to pay for it. The term _________ signifies the ability or the willingness to buy a particular commodity at a given point of time .

a. Market system
b. Discretionary spending
c. Market dominance
d. Demand

26. In economics, the _________ can be defined as the graph depicting the relationship between the price of a certain commodity, and the amount of it that consumers are willing and able to purchase at that given price. It is a graphic representation of a demand schedule The _________ for all consumers together follows from the _________ of every individual consumer: the individual demands at each price are added together.

_________s are used to estimate behaviors in competitive markets, and are often combined with supply curves to estimate the equilibrium price (the price at which sellers together are willing to sell the same amount as buyers together are willing to buy, also known as market clearing price) and the equilibrium quantity (the amount of that good or service that will be produced and bought without surplus/excess supply or shortage/excess demand) of that market.

a. 6-3-5 Brainwriting
b. 180SearchAssistant
c. Power III
d. Demand curve

27. Maslow's _________ is a theory in psychology, proposed by Abraham Maslow in his 1943 paper A Theory of Human Motivation, which he subsequently extended to include his observations of humans' innate curiosity.

Maslow studied what he called exemplary people such as Albert Einstein, Jane Addams, Eleanor Roosevelt, and Frederick Douglass rather than mentally ill or neurotic people, writing that 'the study of crippled, stunted, immature, and unhealthy specimens can yield only a cripple psychology and a cripple philosophy.' Maslow also studied the healthiest one percent of the college student population. In his book, The Farther Reaches of Human Nature, Maslow writes, 'By ordinary standards of this kind of laboratory research...

a. Power III
b. Hierarchy of needs
c. 180SearchAssistant
d. 6-3-5 Brainwriting

28. In environmental modeling and especially in hydrology, a _________ model means a model that is acceptably consistent with observed natural processes, i.e. that simulates well, for example, observed river discharge. It is a key concept of the so-called Generalized Likelihood Uncertainty Estimation (GLUE) methodology to quantify how uncertain environmental predictions are.

a. Behavioral
b. Power III
c. 6-3-5 Brainwriting
d. 180SearchAssistant

29. Cognition is the scientific term for 'the process of thought.' Its usage varies in different ways in accord with different disciplines: For example, in psychology and _________ science it refers to an information processing view of an individual's psychological functions. Other interpretations of the meaning of cognition link it to the development of concepts; individual minds, groups, organizations, and even larger coalitions of entities, can be modelled as 'societies' (Society of Mind), which cooperate to form concepts.

The autonomous elements of each 'society' would have the opportunity to demonstrate emergent behavior in the face of some crisis or opportunity.

a. 6-3-5 Brainwriting
b. Cognitive
c. 180SearchAssistant
d. Power III

30. In psychology, philosophy, and the cognitive sciences, _________ is the process of attaining awareness or understanding of sensory information. It is a task far more complex than was imagined in the 1950s and 1960s, when it was predicted that building perceiving machines would take about a decade, a goal which is still very far from fruition. The word _________ comes from the Latin words _________, percepio, meaning 'receiving, collecting, action of taking possession, apprehension with the mind or senses.'

_________ is one of the oldest fields in psychology.

a. Perception
b. Groupthink
c. 180SearchAssistant
d. Power III

31. _________ is difficult to define. For example, in 1952, Alfred Kroeber and Clyde Kluckhohn compiled a list of 164 definitions of '_________' in _________: A Critical Review of Concepts and Definitions. However, the word '_________' is most commonly used in three basic senses:

- excellence of taste in the fine arts and humanities
- an integrated pattern of human knowledge, belief, and behavior that depends upon the capacity for symbolic thought and social learning
- the set of shared attitudes, values, goals, and practices that characterizes an institution, organization or group.

When the concept first emerged in eighteenth- and nineteenth-century Europe, it connoted a process of cultivation or improvement, as in agriculture or horticulture. In the nineteenth century, it came to refer first to the betterment or refinement of the individual, especially through education, and then to the fulfillment of national aspirations or ideals.

a. African Americans
b. Albert Einstein
c. AStore
d. Culture

32. A _________ is a sociological concept referring to a group to which an individual or another group is compared.

_________s are used in order to evaluate and determine the nature of a given individual or other group's characteristics and sociological attributes. It is the group to which the individual relates or aspires relate himself or self psychologically.

a. Minority
b. Power III
c. Reference group
d. Mociology

33. _________ , according to The American Marketing Association, is 'a planning process designed to assure that all brand contacts received by a customer or prospect for a product, service, or organization are relevant to that person and consistent over time.' (Marketing Power Dictionary)

_________ is a term used to describe a holistic approach to marketing. It aims to ensure consistency of message and the complementary use of media. The concept includes online and offline marketing channels.

a. ADTECH
b. AMAX
c. ACNielsen
d. Integrated marketing communications

34. _________ involves disseminating information about a product, product line, brand, or company. It is one of the four key aspects of the marketing mix. (The other three elements are product marketing, pricing, and distribution). P>_________ is generally sub-divided into two parts:

- Above the line _________: Promotion in the media (e.g. TV, radio, newspapers, Internet and Mobile Phones) in which the advertiser pays an advertising agency to place the ad
- Below the line _________: All other _________. Much of this is intended to be subtle enough for the consumer to be unaware that _________ is taking place. E.g. sponsorship, product placement, endorsements, sales _________, merchandising, direct mail, personal selling, public relations, trade shows

a. Bottling lines
b. Davie Brown Index
c. Cashmere Agency
d. Promotion

35. _________ is a method of direct marketing in which a salesperson solicits to prospective customers to buy products or services, either over the phone or through a subsequent face to face or Web conferencing appointment scheduled during the call.

_________ can also include recorded sales pitches programmed to be played over the phone via automatic dialing. _________ has come under fire in recent years, being viewed as an annoyance by many.

a. Phishing
b. Telemarketing
c. Directory Harvest Attack
d. Joe job

36. _________ is defined by the American _________ Association as the activity, set of institutions, and processes for creating, communicating, delivering, and exchanging offerings that have value for customers, clients, partners, and society at large. The term developed from the original meaning which referred literally to going to market, as in shopping, or going to a market to sell goods or services.

_________ practice tends to be seen as a creative industry, which includes advertising, distribution and selling.

a. Marketing myopia
b. Customer acquisition management
c. Marketing
d. Product naming

37. _________ refers to messages and related media used to communicate with a market. Those who practice advertising, branding, direct marketing, graphic design, marketing, packaging, promotion, publicity, sponsorship, public relations, sales, sales promotion and online marketing are termed marketing communicators, _________ managers, or more briefly as marcom managers.

a. Sales promotion
b. Merchandising
c. Merchandise
d. Marketing communication

1. _________ is a term in economics, where demand for one good or service occurs as a result of demand for another. This may occur as the former is a part of production of the second. For example, demand for coal leads to _________ for mining, as coal must be mined for coal to be consumed.

a. 180SearchAssistant
b. Power III
c. 6-3-5 Brainwriting
d. Derived demand

2. A _________, in marketing, procurement, and organizational studies, is a group of employees, family members, or members of any type of organization responsible for purchasing an item for the organization. In a business setting, major purchases typically require input from various parts of the organization, including finance, accounting, purchasing, information technology management, and senior management. Highly technical purchases, such as information systems or production equipment, also require the expertise of technical specialists.

a. Packshot
b. Marketing myopia
c. Commercialization
d. Buying center

3. In economics, _________ is the desire to own something and the ability to pay for it. The term _________ signifies the ability or the willingness to buy a particular commodity at a given point of time .

.

a. Discretionary spending
b. Market dominance
c. Market system
d. Demand

4. _________ is defined by the American _________ Association as the activity, set of institutions, and processes for creating, communicating, delivering, and exchanging offerings that have value for customers, clients, partners, and society at large. The term developed from the original meaning which referred literally to going to market, as in shopping, or going to a market to sell goods or services.

_________ practice tends to be seen as a creative industry, which includes advertising, distribution and selling.

a. Marketing
b. Marketing myopia
c. Product naming
d. Customer acquisition management

5. A _________ is a type of wholesale merchant business that buys goods and bulk products from importers, other wholesalers and then sells to retailers. _________s can deal in any commodity destined for the retail market. Typical categories are food, lumber, hardware, fuel, and textiles.

a. Tacit collusion
b. Refusal to deal
c. Chief privacy officer
d. Jobbing house

6. A _________ is a company or individual that purchases goods or services with the intention of reselling them rather than consuming or using them. This is usually done for profit (but could be resold at a loss.) One example can be found in the industry of telecommunications, where companies buy excess amounts of transmission capacity or call time from other carriers and resell it to smaller carriers.

a. Reseller
b. Jobbing house
c. Value-based pricing
d. Discontinuation

7. An _________ is the manufacturing of a good or service within a category. Although _________ is a broad term for any kind of economic production, in economics and urban planning _________ is a synonym for the secondary sector, which is a type of economic activity involved in the manufacturing of raw materials into goods and products.

There are four key industrial economic sectors: the primary sector, largely raw material extraction industries such as mining and farming; the secondary sector, involving refining, construction, and manufacturing; the tertiary sector, which deals with services (such as law and medicine) and distribution of manufactured goods; and the quaternary sector, a relatively new type of knowledge _________ focusing on technological research, design and development such as computer programming, and biochemistry.

a. ACNielsen
b. Industry
c. AMAX
d. ADTECH

8. The _________ or _________ is used by business and government to classify and measure economic activity in Canada, Mexico and the United States. It has largely replaced the older Standard Industrial Classification system; however, certain government departments and agencies, such as the U.S. Securities and Exchange Commission (SEC), still use the SIC codes.

The _________ numbering system is a six-digit code.

a. 6-3-5 Brainwriting
b. North American Industry Classification System
c. 180SearchAssistant
d. Power III

9. _________ is an advertisement in which a particular product specifically mentions a competitor by name for the express purpose of showing why the competitor is inferior to the product naming it.

This should not be confused with parody advertisements, where a fictional product is being advertised for the purpose of poking fun at the particular advertisement, nor should it be confused with the use of a coined brand name for the purpose of comparing the product without actually naming an actual competitor. ('Wikipedia tastes better and is less filling than the Encyclopedia Galactica.')

In the 1980s, during what has been referred to as the cola wars, soft-drink manufacturer Pepsi ran a series of advertisements where people, caught on hidden camera, in a blind taste test, chose Pepsi over rival Coca-Cola.

a. Heavy-up
b. GL-70
c. Cost per conversion
d. Comparative advertising

10. In business and engineering, new _________ is the term used to describe the complete process of bringing a new product or service to market. There are two parallel paths involved in the Nproduct development process: one involves the idea generation, product design, and detail engineering; the other involves market research and marketing analysis. Companies typically see new _________ as the first stage in generating and commercializing new products within the overall strategic process of product life cycle management used to maintain or grow their market share.

a. Specification tree
b. New product development
c. New product screening
d. Product development

11. A _________ is an invitation for suppliers, often through a bidding process, to submit a proposal on a specific commodity or service. A bidding process is one of the best methods for leveraging a company's negotiating ability and purchasing power with suppliers. The _________ process brings structure to the procurement decision and allows the risks and benefits to be identified clearly upfront.

a. Request for proposal
b. Hit rate
c. Lead generation
d. Sales management

12. A _________ is an explicit set of requirements to be satisfied by a material, product, or service.

In engineering, manufacturing, and business, it is vital for suppliers, purchasers, and users of materials, products, or services to understand and agree upon all requirements. A _________ is a type of a standard which is often referenced by a contract or procurement document.

a. Specification
b. Product optimization
c. Product development
d. New product development

13. In economics ' business, specifically cost accounting, the _________ is the point at which cost or expenses and revenue are equal: there is no net loss or gain, and one has 'broken even'. A profit or a loss has not been made, although opportunity costs have been paid, and capital has received the risk-adjusted, expected return.

For example, if the business sells less than 200 tables each month, it will make a loss, if it sells more, it will be a profit.

a. 180SearchAssistant
b. Power III
c. Total revenue
d. Break-even point

14. _________ is an idea in the field of Organizational studies and management which describes the psychology, attitudes, experiences, beliefs and Values (personal and cultural values)of an organization. It has been defined as 'the specific collection of values and norms that are shared by people and groups in an organization and that control the way they interact with each other and with stakeholders outside the organization.'

This definition continues to explain organizational values also known as 'beliefs and ideas about what kinds of goals members of an organization should pursue and ideas about the appropriate kinds or standards of behavior organizational members should use to achieve these goals. From organizational values develop organizational norms, guidelines or expectations that prescribe appropriate kinds of behavior by employees in particular situations and control the behavior of organizational members towards one another.'

_________ is not the same as corporate culture.

a. Organizational structure
b. ADTECH
c. ACNielsen
d. Organizational culture

15. _________ is difficult to define. For example, in 1952, Alfred Kroeber and Clyde Kluckhohn compiled a list of 164 definitions of '_________' in _________: A Critical Review of Concepts and Definitions. However, the word '_________' is most commonly used in three basic senses:

- excellence of taste in the fine arts and humanities
- an integrated pattern of human knowledge, belief, and behavior that depends upon the capacity for symbolic thought and social learning
- the set of shared attitudes, values, goals, and practices that characterizes an institution, organization or group.

When the concept first emerged in eighteenth- and nineteenth-century Europe, it connoted a process of cultivation or improvement, as in agriculture or horticulture. In the nineteenth century, it came to refer first to the betterment or refinement of the individual, especially through education, and then to the fulfillment of national aspirations or ideals.

a. AStore
b. Albert Einstein
c. African Americans
d. Culture

16. _________ is one of the four growth strategies of the Product-Market Growth Matrix defined by Ansoff. _________ occurs when a company enters/penetrates a market with current products. The best way to achieve this is by gaining competitors' customers (part of their market share.)

a. Horizontal market
b. Marketization
c. Pasar pagi
d. Market penetration

17. A _________ is a tool used in industrial business-to-business procurement. It is a type of auction in which the role of the buyer and seller are reversed, with the primary objective to drive purchase prices downward. In an ordinary auction, buyers compete to obtain a good or service.

a. Vendor Managed Inventory
b. Fulfillment house
c. Materials management
d. Reverse auction

18. _________ is a form of communication that typically attempts to persuade potential customers to purchase or to consume more of a particular brand of product or service. 'While now central to the contemporary global economy and the reproduction of global production networks, it is only quite recently that _________ has been more than a marginal influence on patterns of sales and production. The formation of modern _________ was intimately bound up with the emergence of new forms of monopoly capitalism around the end of the 19th and beginning of the 20th century as one element in corporate strategies to create, organize and where possible control markets, especially for mass produced consumer goods.

a. ADTECH
b. ACNielsen
c. Advertising
d. AMAX

1. The Oxford University Press defines _________ as 'marketing on a worldwide scale reconciling or taking commercial advantage of global operational differences, similarities and opportunities in order to meet global objectives.' Oxford University Press' Glossary of Marketing Terms.

Here are three reasons for the shift from domestic to _________ as given by the authors of the textbook, _________ Management--3rd Edition by Masaaki Kotabe and Kristiaan Helsen, 2004.

One of the product categories in which global competition has been easy to track is in U.S. automotive sales.

a. Diversity marketing
b. Digital marketing
c. Guerrilla Marketing
d. Global marketing

2. _________ is defined by the American _________ Association as the activity, set of institutions, and processes for creating, communicating, delivering, and exchanging offerings that have value for customers, clients, partners, and society at large. The term developed from the original meaning which referred literally to going to market, as in shopping, or going to a market to sell goods or services.

_________ practice tends to be seen as a creative industry, which includes advertising, distribution and selling.

a. Marketing myopia
b. Product naming
c. Customer acquisition management
d. Marketing

3. _________ in its literal sense is the process of transformation of local or regional phenomena into global ones. It can be described as a process by which the people of the world are unified into a single society and function together.

This process is a combination of economic, technological, sociocultural and political forces.

a. 180SearchAssistant
b. Power III
c. Globalization
d. 6-3-5 Brainwriting

4. The General Agreement on Tariffs and Trade was the outcome of the failure of negotiating governments to create the International Trade Organization (ITO.) _________ was formed in 1947 and lasted until 1994, when it was replaced by the World Trade Organization. The Bretton Woods Conference had introduced the idea for an organization to regulate trade as part of a larger plan for economic recovery after World War II.

a. Power III
b. General Agreement on Tariffs and Trade
c. Trade pact
d. GATT

5. The _________ is an international financial institution that provides financial and technical assistance to developing countries for development programs (e.g. bridges, roads, schools, etc.) with the stated goal of reducing poverty.

The _________ differs from the _________ Group, in that the _________ comprises only two institutions:

- International Bank for Reconstruction and Development (IBRD)
- International Development Association (IDA)

Whereas the latter incorporates these two in addition to three more:

- International Finance Corporation (IFC)
- Multilateral Investment Guarantee Agency (MIGA)
- International Centre for Settlement of Investment Disputes (ICSID)

John Maynard Keynes (right) represented the UK at the conference, and Harry Dexter White represented the US.

The _________ was created following the ratification of the United Nations Monetary and Financial Conference of the Bretton Woods agreement. The concept was originally conceived in July 1944 at the United Nations Monetary and Financial Conference.

a. 180SearchAssistant
b. 6-3-5 Brainwriting
c. Power III
d. World Bank

6. _________s is the social science that studies the production, distribution, and consumption of goods and services. The term _________s comes from the Ancient Greek oá¼°κονομÎ¯α from oá¼¶κος (oikos, 'house') + νÏŒμος (nomos, 'custom' or 'law'), hence 'rules of the house(hold)'. Current _________ models developed out of the broader field of political economy in the late 19th century, owing to a desire to use an empirical approach more akin to the physical sciences.

a. Industrial organization
b. Economic
c. ADTECH
d. ACNielsen

7. An _________ is a situation that will often involve an apparent conflict between moral imperatives, in which to obey one would result in transgressing another. This is also called an ethical paradox since in moral philosophy, paradox plays a central role in ethics debates. For instance, an ethical admonition to 'love thy neighbour as thy self' is not always just in contrast with, but sometimes in contradiction to an armed neighbour actively trying to kill you: if he or she succeeds, you will not be able to love him or her.

a. ACNielsen
b. Ethical dilemma
c. AMAX
d. ADTECH

8. _________ is systematic determination of merit, worth, and significance of something or someone using criteria against a set of standards. _________ often is used to characterize and appraise subjects of interest in a wide range of human enterprises, including the arts, criminal justice, foundations and non-profit organizations, government, health care, and other human services.

Depending on the topic of interest, there are professional groups which look to the quality and rigor of the _________ process.

a. ADTECH
b. ACNielsen
c. AMAX
d. Evaluation

9. The _________ or gross domestic income (GDI) is one of the measures of national income and output for a given country's economy. It is the total value of all final goods and services produced in a particular economy; the dollar value of all goods and services produced within a country's borders in a given year. _________ can be defined in three ways, all of which are conceptually identical.

a. Microeconomics
b. Gross domestic product
c. Macroeconomics
d. Leading indicator

10. _________ is a term used in Internet marketing to define a popular pricing model whereby a marketing agency will receive a bounty from an advertiser for each new lead or new customer obtained for the advertiser through the agency's online marketing efforts. The agency creates advertising campaigns and promotions to convert the maximum number of new leads or customers and gets paid for its work only when a new lead or a new customer is passed on to the advertiser.

PPP advertising became popular with the advent of the world wide web that allows real time measurement of an advertising campaign's ROI (return on investment.)

a. 6-3-5 Brainwriting
b. 180SearchAssistant
c. Power III
d. Pay for performance advertising

11. _________ is a form of communication that typically attempts to persuade potential customers to purchase or to consume more of a particular brand of product or service. 'While now central to the contemporary global economy and the reproduction of global production networks, it is only quite recently that _________ has been more than a marginal influence on patterns of sales and production. The formation of modern _________ was intimately bound up with the emergence of new forms of monopoly capitalism around the end of the 19th and beginning of the 20th century as one element in corporate strategies to create, organize and where possible control markets, especially for mass produced consumer goods.

a. ACNielsen
b. ADTECH
c. AMAX
d. Advertising

12. An _________ is a series of advertisement messages that share a single idea and theme which make up an integrated marketing communication (IMC.) _________s appear in different media across a specific time frame.

The critical part of making an _________ is determining a campaign theme, as it sets the tone for the individual advertisements and other forms of marketing communications that will be used.

a. AMAX
b. Advertising campaign
c. ACNielsen
d. ADTECH

13. In economics ' business, specifically cost accounting, the _________ is the point at which cost or expenses and revenue are equal: there is no net loss or gain, and one has 'broken even'. A profit or a loss has not been made, although opportunity costs have been paid, and capital has received the risk-adjusted, expected return.

For example, if the business sells less than 200 tables each month, it will make a loss, if it sells more, it will be a profit.

a. 180SearchAssistant
b. Power III
c. Total revenue
d. Break-even point

14. _________ or _________ data refers to selected population characteristics as used in government, marketing or opinion research, or the _________ profiles used in such research. Note the distinction from the term 'demography' Commonly-used _________ include race, age, income, disabilities, mobility (in terms of travel time to work or number of vehicles available), educational attainment, home ownership, employment status, and even location.

a. African Americans
b. AStore
c. Albert Einstein
d. Demographic

15. _________ is the change in population over time, and can be quantified as the change in the number of individuals in a population using 'per unit time' for measurement. The term _________ can technically refer to any species, but almost always refers to humans, and it is often used informally for the more specific demographic term _________ rate , and is often used to refer specifically to the growth of the population of the world.

Simple models of _________ include the Malthusian Growth Model and the logistic model.

a. 180SearchAssistant
b. Power III
c. Population growth
d. 6-3-5 Brainwriting

16. A _________ is a tax imposed on goods when they are moved across a political boundary. They are usually associated with protectionism, the economic policy of restraining trade between nations. For political reasons, _________s are usually imposed on imported goods, although they may also be imposed on exported goods.

a. Fiscal policy
b. Monetary policy
c. Power III
d. Tariff

17. In economics, '_________' can refer to any kind of predatory pricing. However, the word is now generally used only in the context of international trade law, where _________ is defined as the act of a manufacturer in one country exporting a product to another country at a price which is either below the price it charges in its home market or is below its costs of production. The term has a negative connotation, but advocates of free markets see '_________' as beneficial for consumers and believe that protectionism to prevent it would have net negative consequences.

a. Gold Key Matching Service
b. Sample sales
c. Dumping
d. Hawkers

18. _________ is exchanging goods or services that are paid for, in whole or part, with other goods or services.

There are five main variants of _________:

- Barter: Exchange of goods or services directly for other goods or services without the use of money as means of purchase or payment.
- Switch trading: Practice in which one company sells to another its obligation to make a purchase in a given country.
- Counter purchase: Sale of goods and services to a country by a company that promises to make a future purchase of a specific product from the country.
- Buyback: occurs when a firm builds a plant in a country - or supplies technology, equipment, training, or other services to the country and agrees to take a certain percentage of the plant's output as partial payment for the contract.
- Offset: Agreement that a company will offset a hard - currency purchase of an unspecified product from that nation in the future. Agreement by one nation to buy a product from another, subject to the purchase of some or all of the components and raw materials from the buyer of the finished product, or the assembly of such product in the buyer nation.

a. Countertrade
b. Merchant
c. RFM
d. Retail loss prevention

19. In finance, the _________s between two currencies specifies how much one currency is worth in terms of the other. It is the value of a foreign nation's currency in terms of the home nation's currency. For example an _________ of 102 Japanese yen to the United States dollar means that JPY 102 is worth the same as USD 1.

a. ACNielsen
b. AMAX
c. ADTECH
d. Exchange rate

20. The _________ is an economic and political union of 27 member states, located primarily in Europe. It was established by the Treaty of Maastricht on 1 November 1993 upon the foundations of the pre-existing European Economic Community. With almost 500 million citizens, the _________ combined generates an estimated 30% share (US$16.8 trillion in 2007) of the nominal gross world product.

a. ACNielsen
b. Eurozone
c. ADTECH
d. European Union

21. _________ is a broad label that refers to any individuals or households that use goods and services generated within the economy. The concept of a _________ is used in different contexts, so that the usage and significance of the term may vary.

A _________ is a person who uses any product or service.

a. Consumer
b. 6-3-5 Brainwriting
c. Power III
d. 180SearchAssistant

22. _________ is a form of government regulation which protects the interests of consumers. For example, a government may require businesses to disclose detailed information about products--particularly in areas where safety or public health is an issue, such as food. _________ is linked to the idea of consumer rights (that consumers have various rights as consumers), and to the formation of consumer organizations which help consumers make better choices in the marketplace.

a. Trademark dilution
b. Sound trademark
c. Federal Bureau of Investigation
d. Consumer protection

23. A _________ is a wide ranging tax, tariff and _________ that often includes investment guarantees. _________s are frequently politically contentious since they may change economic customs and deepen interdependence with trade partners. Increasing efficiency through 'free trade' is a common goal.

a. General Agreement on Trade in Services
b. Trade pact
c. Power III
d. General Agreement on Tariffs and Trade

24. The _________ is a trilateral trade bloc in North America created by the governments of the United States, Canada, and Mexico. It superseded the Canada-United States Free Trade Agreement between the US and Canada.

Following diplomatic negotiations dating back to 1990 between the three nations, the leaders met in San Antonio, Texas on December 17, 1992 to sign _________.

a. 180SearchAssistant
b. North American Free Trade Agreement
c. 6-3-5 Brainwriting
d. Power III

25. _________ is difficult to define. For example, in 1952, Alfred Kroeber and Clyde Kluckhohn compiled a list of 164 definitions of '_________' in _________: A Critical Review of Concepts and Definitions. However, the word '_________' is most commonly used in three basic senses:

- excellence of taste in the fine arts and humanities
- an integrated pattern of human knowledge, belief, and behavior that depends upon the capacity for symbolic thought and social learning
- the set of shared attitudes, values, goals, and practices that characterizes an institution, organization or group.

When the concept first emerged in eighteenth- and nineteenth-century Europe, it connoted a process of cultivation or improvement, as in agriculture or horticulture. In the nineteenth century, it came to refer first to the betterment or refinement of the individual, especially through education, and then to the fulfillment of national aspirations or ideals.

a. African Americans
b. Albert Einstein
c. Culture
d. AStore

26. _________ can be regarded as an outcome of mental processes (cognitive process) leading to the selection of a course of action among several alternatives. Every _________ process produces a final choice. The output can be an action or an opinion of choice.

a. 6-3-5 Brainwriting
b. Decision making
c. 180SearchAssistant
d. Power III

27. A personal and cultural _________ is a relative ethic _________, an assumption upon which implementation can be extrapolated. A _________ system is a set of consistent _________s and measures that is soo not true. A principle _________ is a foundation upon which other _________s and measures of integrity are based.

a. Supreme Court of the United States
b. Package-on-Package
c. Perceptual maps
d. Value

28. _________ is exchange of capital, goods, and services across international borders or territories. In most countries, it represents a significant share of gross domestic product (GDP.) While _________ has been present throughout much of history , its economic, social, and political importance has been on the rise in recent centuries.

a. ACNielsen
b. Incoterms
c. ADTECH
d. International trade

29. _________ refers to the methods of practicing and using another person's philosophy of business. The franchisor grants the independent operator the right to distribute its products, techniques, and trademarks for a percentage of gross monthly sales and a royalty fee. Various tangibles and intangibles such as national or international advertising, training, and other support services are commonly made available by the franchisor.

a. 180SearchAssistant
b. Franchise fee
c. Power III
d. Franchising

30. The _________ is generally accepted as the use and specification of the four p's describing the strategic position of a product in the marketplace. One version of the origins of the _________ starts in 1948 when James Culliton said that a marketing decision should be a result of something similar to a recipe. This version continued in 1953 when Neil Borden, in his American Marketing Association presidential address, took the recipe idea one step further and coined the term 'Marketing-Mix'.

a. Power III
b. 180SearchAssistant
c. 6-3-5 Brainwriting
d. Marketing mix

31. A _________ is an entity formed between two or more parties to undertake economic activity together. The parties agree to create a new entity by both contributing equity, and they then share in the revenues, expenses, and control of the enterprise. The venture can be for one specific project only, or a continuing business relationship such as the Fuji Xerox _________.

a. Consumer protection
b. Joint venture
c. Trademark attorney
d. Gripe site

32. Foreign _________ in its classic form is defined as a company from one country making a physical investment into building a factory in another country. It is the establishment of an enterprise by a foreigner. Its definition can be extended to include investments made to acquire lasting interest in enterprises operating outside of the economy of the investor.

a. Fountain Fresh International
b. VideoJug
c. Brash Brands
d. Direct investment

33. A _________ is a process that can allow an organization to concentrate its limited resources on the greatest opportunities to increase sales and achieve a sustainable competitive advantage. A _________ should be centered around the key concept that customer satisfaction is the main goal.

A _________ is most effective when it is an integral component of corporate strategy, defining how the organization will successfully engage customers, prospects, and competitors in the market arena.

a. Psychographic
b. Marketing strategy
c. Cyberdoc
d. Societal marketing

34. In marketing, _________ has come to mean the process by which marketers try to create an image or identity in the minds of their target market for its product, brand, or organization. It is the 'relative competitive comparison' their product occupies in a given market as perceived by the target market.

Re-_________ involves changing the identity of a product, relative to the identity of competing products, in the collective minds of the target market.

a. GE matrix
b. Positioning
c. Moratorium
d. Containerization

35. In marketing and advertising, a _________ usually an advertising campaign, is aimed at appealing to. A _________ can be people of a certain age group, gender, marital status, etc. (ex: teenagers, females, single people, etc.)

a. Targeted advertising
b. Brand Development Index
c. National brand
d. Target audience

36. _________ in organizations and public policy is both the organizational process of creating and maintaining a plan; and the psychological process of thinking about the activities required to create a desired goal on some scale. As such, it is a fundamental property of intelligent behavior. This thought process is essential to the creation and refinement of a plan, or integration of it with other plans, that is, it combines forecasting of developments with the preparation of scenarios of how to react to them.

a. 180SearchAssistant
b. 6-3-5 Brainwriting
c. Planning
d. Power III

37. In business and engineering, new _________ is the term used to describe the complete process of bringing a new product or service to market. There are two parallel paths involved in the Nproduct development process: one involves the idea generation, product design, and detail engineering; the other involves market research and marketing analysis. Companies typically see new _________ as the first stage in generating and commercializing new products within the overall strategic process of product life cycle management used to maintain or grow their market share.

a. Specification tree
b. New product development
c. New product screening
d. Product development

38. _________ is an advertisement in which a particular product specifically mentions a competitor by name for the express purpose of showing why the competitor is inferior to the product naming it.

This should not be confused with parody advertisements, where a fictional product is being advertised for the purpose of poking fun at the particular advertisement, nor should it be confused with the use of a coined brand name for the purpose of comparing the product without actually naming an actual competitor. ('Wikipedia tastes better and is less filling than the Encyclopedia Galactica.')

In the 1980s, during what has been referred to as the cola wars, soft-drink manufacturer Pepsi ran a series of advertisements where people, caught on hidden camera, in a blind taste test, chose Pepsi over rival Coca-Cola.

a. Cost per conversion
b. GL-70
c. Heavy-up
d. Comparative advertising

39. _________ is one of the four Ps of the marketing mix. The other three aspects are product, promotion, and place. It is also a key variable in microeconomic price allocation theory.

a. Price
b. Pricing
c. Relationship based pricing
d. Competitor indexing

40. _________ is one of the four elements of marketing mix. An organization or set of organizations (go-betweens) involved in the process of making a product or service available for use or consumption by a consumer or business user.

The other three parts of the marketing mix are product, pricing, and promotion.

a. Better Living Through Chemistry
b. Comparison-Shopping agent
c. Japan Advertising Photographers' Association
d. Distribution

41. _________ is a branch of philosophy which seeks to address questions about morality, such as how a moral outcome can be achieved in a specific situation (applied _________), how moral values should be determined (normative _________), what moral values people actually abide by (descriptive _________), what the fundamental semantic, ontological, and epistemic nature of _________ or morality is (meta-_________), and how moral capacity or moral agency develops and what its nature is (moral psychology.)

Socrates was one of the first Greek philosophers to encourage both scholars and the common citizen to turn their attention from the outside world to the condition of man. In this view, Knowledge having a bearing on human life was placed highest, all other knowledge being secondary.

a. AMAX
b. ADTECH
c. Ethics
d. ACNielsen

42. _________ is the area of applied ethics which deals with the moral principles behind the operation and regulation of marketing. Some areas of _________ overlap with media ethics.

Possible frameworks:

- Value-oriented framework, analyzing ethical problems on the basis of the values which they infringe (e.g. honesty, autonomy, privacy, transparency.) An example of such an approach is the AMA Statement of Ethics.
- Stakeholder-oriented framework, analysing ethical problems on the basis of whom they affect (e.g. consumers, competitors, society as a whole.)
- Process-oriented framework, analysing ethical problems in terms of the categories used by marketing specialists (e.g. research, price, promotion, placement.)

None of these frameworks allows, by itself, a convenient and complete categorization of the great variety of issues in _________.

Contrary to popular impressions, not all marketing is adversarial, and not all marketing is stacked in favour of the marketer.

a. 6-3-5 Brainwriting
b. 180SearchAssistant
c. Marketing Ethics
d. Power III

43. _________ is the practice of promoting, distinguishing, separating, or artificially injecting the culture of one society into another. It is usually the case that the former belongs to a large, economically or militarily powerful nation and the latter belongs to a smaller, less important one. _________ can take the form of an active, formal policy or a general attitude.

a. Power III
b. 6-3-5 Brainwriting
c. 180SearchAssistant
d. Cultural imperialism

44. In economics, an _________ is any good or commodity, transported from one country to another country in a legitimate fashion, typically for use in trade. _________ goods or services are provided to foreign consumers by domestic producers. _________ is an important part of international trade.

a. AMAX
b. ACNielsen
c. Export
d. ADTECH

1. In marketing, _________ has come to mean the process by which marketers try to create an image or identity in the minds of their target market for its product, brand, or organization. It is the 'relative competitive comparison' their product occupies in a given market as perceived by the target market.

Re-_________ involves changing the identity of a product, relative to the identity of competing products, in the collective minds of the target market.

a. Positioning
b. GE matrix
c. Containerization
d. Moratorium

2. _________ is a market coverage strategy in which a firm decides to ignore market segment differences and go after the whole market with one offer.it is type of marketing (or attempting to sell through persuasion) of a product to a wide audience. The idea is to broadcast a message that will reach the largest number of people possible. Traditionally _________ has focused on radio, television and newspapers as the medium used to reach this broad audience.

a. Mass marketing
b. Business-to-consumer
c. Cyberdoc
d. Marketspace

3. _________ is defined by the American _________ Association as the activity, set of institutions, and processes for creating, communicating, delivering, and exchanging offerings that have value for customers, clients, partners, and society at large. The term developed from the original meaning which referred literally to going to market, as in shopping, or going to a market to sell goods or services.

_________ practice tends to be seen as a creative industry, which includes advertising, distribution and selling.

a. Product naming
b. Customer acquisition management
c. Marketing
d. Marketing myopia

4. A _________ is a plan of action designed to achieve a particular goal.

_________ is different from tactics. In military terms, tactics is concerned with the conduct of an engagement while _________ is concerned with how different engagements are linked.

a. Strategy
b. Power III
c. 6-3-5 Brainwriting
d. 180SearchAssistant

5. _________, in marketing, manufacturing, and management, is the use of flexible computer-aided manufacturing systems to produce custom output. Those systems combine the low unit costs of mass production processes with the flexibility of individual customization.

'_________' is the new frontier in business competition for both manufacturing and service industries.

a. Vertical integration
b. Flanking marketing warfare strategies
c. Power III
d. Mass customization

6. _________ is the practice of tailoring products, brands (microbrands), and promotions to meet the needs and wants of microsegments within a market. It is a type of market customization that deals with pricing of customer/product combinations at the store or individual level.

Standard pricing policy ignores the differences in customer segments of specific stores within a regional chain of stores.

a. Chief privacy officer
b. Soft sell
c. Discontinuation
d. Micromarketing

7. _________ refers to marketing strategies applied directly to a specific consumer.

Having the knowledge on the consumer preferences, there are suggested personalized products and promotions to each consumer.

The _________ is based in four main steps in order to fulfill its goals: Those stages are identify, differentiate, interact, and customize.

a. AMAX
b. One-to-one marketing
c. ACNielsen
d. ADTECH

8. On an intranet or B2E Enterprise Web portals, personalization is often based on user attributes such as department, functional area, or role. The term _________ in this context refers to the ability of users to modify the page layout or specify what content should be displayed.

There are two categories of personalizations:

1. Rule-based
2. Content-based

Web personalization models include rules-based filtering, based on 'if this, then that' rules processing, and collaborative filtering, which serves relevant material to customers by combining their own personal preferences with the preferences of like-minded others. Collaborative filtering works well for books, music, video, etc.

a. Self branding
b. Cashmere Agency
c. Customization
d. Movin'

9. _________ or _________ data refers to selected population characteristics as used in government, marketing or opinion research, or the _________ profiles used in such research. Note the distinction from the term 'demography' Commonly-used _________ include race, age, income, disabilities, mobility (in terms of travel time to work or number of vehicles available), educational attainment, home ownership, employment status, and even location.

a. African Americans
b. Demographic
c. AStore
d. Albert Einstein

10. _________ is the study of the Earth and its lands, features, inhabitants, and phenomena. A literal translation would be 'to describe or write about the Earth'. The first person to use the word '_________' was Eratosthenes .

a. Geography
b. 6-3-5 Brainwriting
c. 180SearchAssistant
d. Power III

11. _________ was originally coined by Austrian psychologist Alfred Adler in 1929. The current broader sense of the word dates from 1961.

In sociology, a _________ is the way a person lives.

a. Power III
b. 180SearchAssistant
c. 6-3-5 Brainwriting
d. Lifestyle

12. _________ or self identity refers to the global understanding a sentient being has of him or herself. It presupposes but can be distinguished from self-consciousness, which is simply an awareness of one's self. It is also more general than self-esteem, which is the purely evaluative element of the _________.

a. 180SearchAssistant
b. Need for cognition
c. Self-concept
d. Power III

13. A personal and cultural _________ is a relative ethic _________, an assumption upon which implementation can be extrapolated. A _________ system is a set of consistent _________s and measures that is soo not true. A principle _________ is a foundation upon which other _________s and measures of integrity are based.

a. Value
b. Package-on-Package
c. Perceptual maps
d. Supreme Court of the United States

14. Its a tool for marketing. _________ is a multivariate statistical classification technique for discovering whether the individuals of a population fall into different groups by making quantitative comparisons of multiple characteristics with the assumption that the differences within any group should be less than the differences between groups.

The information technologies employed in _________ include geographic information system and database management software.

a. Linear discriminant analysis
b. Principal component analysis
c. Multiple discriminant analysis
d. Geodemographic segmentation

15. _________ is the ability of an individual or group to seclude themselves or information about themselves and thereby reveal themselves selectively. The boundaries and content of what is considered private differ among cultures and individuals, but share basic common themes. _________ is sometimes related to anonymity, the wish to remain unnoticed or unidentified in the public realm.

a. 6-3-5 Brainwriting
b. Power III
c. 180SearchAssistant
d. Privacy

16. In marketing and advertising, a _________ usually an advertising campaign, is aimed at appealing to. A _________ can be people of a certain age group, gender, marital status, etc. (ex: teenagers, females, single people, etc.)

a. Targeted advertising
b. National brand
c. Brand Development Index
d. Target audience

17. A _________ is a collection of symbols, experiences and associations connected with a product, a service, a person or any other artifact or entity.

_________s have become increasingly important components of culture and the economy, now being described as 'cultural accessories and personal philosophies'.

Some people distinguish the psychological aspect of a _________ from the experiential aspect.

a. Brand
b. Brandable software
c. Brand equity
d. Store brand

18. A _________ is a type of department store, which sell products at prices lower than those asked by traditional retail outlets. Most discount department stores offer wide assortments of goods; others specialize in such merchandise as jewelry, electronic equipment, or electrical appliances. _________s are not dollar stores, which sell goods at a dollar or less.

a. Sales per unit area
b. Strip mall
c. Gruen transfer
d. Discount store

19. _________ is a rivalry between individuals, groups, nations for territory, a niche, or allocation of resources. It arises whenever two or more parties strive for a goal which cannot be shared. _________ occurs naturally between living organisms which co-exist in the same environment.

a. Price fixing
b. Competition
c. Non-price competition
d. Price competition

20. An _________ is a situation that will often involve an apparent conflict between moral imperatives, in which to obey one would result in transgressing another. This is also called an ethical paradox since in moral philosophy, paradox plays a central role in ethics debates. For instance, an ethical admonition to 'love thy neighbour as thy self' is not always just in contrast with, but sometimes in contradiction to an armed neighbour actively trying to kill you: if he or she succeeds, you will not be able to love him or her.

a. Ethical dilemma
b. ACNielsen
c. ADTECH
d. AMAX

21. _________ is a fee paid on borrowed assets. It is the price paid for the use of borrowed money , or, money earned by deposited funds . Assets that are sometimes lent with _________ include money, shares, consumer goods through hire purchase, major assets such as aircraft, and even entire factories in finance lease arrangements.

a. Interest
b. ADTECH
c. ACNielsen
d. AMAX

22. In business and engineering, new _________ is the term used to describe the complete process of bringing a new product or service to market. There are two parallel paths involved in the Nproduct development process: one involves the idea generation, product design, and detail engineering; the other involves market research and marketing analysis. Companies typically see new _________ as the first stage in generating and commercializing new products within the overall strategic process of product life cycle management used to maintain or grow their market share.

a. Specification tree
b. New product development
c. New product screening
d. Product development

23. _________ is a form of communication that typically attempts to persuade potential customers to purchase or to consume more of a particular brand of product or service. 'While now central to the contemporary global economy and the reproduction of global production networks, it is only quite recently that _________ has been more than a marginal influence on patterns of sales and production. The formation of modern _________ was intimately bound up with the emergence of new forms of monopoly capitalism around the end of the 19th and beginning of the 20th century as one element in corporate strategies to create, organize and where possible control markets, especially for mass produced consumer goods.

a. AMAX
b. ADTECH
c. ACNielsen
d. Advertising

24. _________ can be regarded as an outcome of mental processes (cognitive process) leading to the selection of a course of action among several alternatives. Every _________ process produces a final choice. The output can be an action or an opinion of choice.

a. Decision making
b. 180SearchAssistant
c. Power III
d. 6-3-5 Brainwriting

25. Perceptual mapping is a graphics technique used by asset marketers that attempts to visually display the perceptions of customers or potential customers. Typically the position of a product, product line, brand, or company is displayed relative to their competition.

_________ can have any number of dimensions but the most common is two dimensions.

a. Developed country
b. Retail floor planning
c. Comparison-Shopping agent
d. Perceptual maps

1. _________ generally refers to a list of all planned expenses and revenues. It is a plan for saving and spending. A _________ is an important concept in microeconomics, which uses a _________ line to illustrate the trade-offs between two or more goods.

a. 180SearchAssistant
b. 6-3-5 Brainwriting
c. Power III
d. Budget

2. _________ is defined by the American _________ Association as the activity, set of institutions, and processes for creating, communicating, delivering, and exchanging offerings that have value for customers, clients, partners, and society at large. The term developed from the original meaning which referred literally to going to market, as in shopping, or going to a market to sell goods or services.

_________ practice tends to be seen as a creative industry, which includes advertising, distribution and selling.

a. Marketing
b. Customer acquisition management
c. Marketing myopia
d. Product naming

3. Consumer market research is a form of applied sociology that concentrates on understanding the behaviours, whims and preferences, of consumers in a market-based economy, and aims to understand the effects and comparative success of marketing campaigns. The field of consumer _________ as a statistical science was pioneered by Arthur Nielsen with the founding of the ACNielsen Company in 1923 .

Thus _________ is the systematic and objective identification, collection, analysis, and dissemination of information for the purpose of assisting management in decision making related to the identification and solution of problems and opportunities in marketing.

a. Marketing research process
b. Logit analysis
c. Focus group
d. Marketing research

4. _________ is a branch of philosophy which seeks to address questions about morality, such as how a moral outcome can be achieved in a specific situation (applied _________), how moral values should be determined (normative _________), what moral values people actually abide by (descriptive _________), what the fundamental semantic, ontological, and epistemic nature of _________ or morality is (meta-_________), and how moral capacity or moral agency develops and what its nature is (moral psychology.)

Socrates was one of the first Greek philosophers to encourage both scholars and the common citizen to turn their attention from the outside world to the condition of man. In this view, Knowledge having a bearing on human life was placed highest, all other knowledge being secondary.

a. AMAX
b. ADTECH
c. ACNielsen
d. Ethics

5. A personal and cultural _________ is a relative ethic _________, an assumption upon which implementation can be extrapolated. A _________ system is a set of consistent _________s and measures that is soo not true. A principle _________ is a foundation upon which other _________s and measures of integrity are based.

a. Package-on-Package
b. Supreme Court of the United States
c. Perceptual maps
d. Value

6. A _________ is a collection of symbols, experiences and associations connected with a product, a service, a person or any other artifact or entity.

_________s have become increasingly important components of culture and the economy, now being described as 'cultural accessories and personal philosophies'.

Some people distinguish the psychological aspect of a _________ from the experiential aspect.

a. Brandable software
b. Brand equity
c. Store brand
d. Brand

7. _________ is a broad label that refers to any individuals or households that use goods and services generated within the economy. The concept of a _________ is used in different contexts, so that the usage and significance of the term may vary.

A _________ is a person who uses any product or service.

a. 180SearchAssistant
b. 6-3-5 Brainwriting
c. Power III
d. Consumer

8. _________ refer to a collection of facts usually collected as the result of experience, observation or experiment or a set of premises. This may consist of numbers, words particularly as measurements or observations of a set of variables. _________ are often viewed as a lowest level of abstraction from which information and knowledge are derived.

a. Sample size
b. Mean
c. Pearson product-moment correlation coefficient
d. Data

9. _________ is the process of extracting hidden patterns from data. As more data is gathered, with the amount of data doubling every three years, _________ is becoming an increasingly important tool to transform this data into information. It is commonly used in a wide range of profiling practices, such as marketing, surveillance, fraud detection and scientific discovery.

a. Data mining
b. 180SearchAssistant
c. Structure mining
d. Power III

10. _________ is the ability of an individual or group to seclude themselves or information about themselves and thereby reveal themselves selectively. The boundaries and content of what is considered private differ among cultures and individuals, but share basic common themes. _________ is sometimes related to anonymity, the wish to remain unnoticed or unidentified in the public realm.

a. Privacy
b. 180SearchAssistant
c. Power III
d. 6-3-5 Brainwriting

11. _________ is a form of communication that typically attempts to persuade potential customers to purchase or to consume more of a particular brand of product or service. 'While now central to the contemporary global economy and the reproduction of global production networks, it is only quite recently that _________ has been more than a marginal influence on patterns of sales and production. The formation of modern _________ was intimately bound up with the emergence of new forms of monopoly capitalism around the end of the 19th and beginning of the 20th century as one element in corporate strategies to create, organize and where possible control markets, especially for mass produced consumer goods.

a. ADTECH
b. AMAX
c. ACNielsen
d. Advertising

12. In economics, _________ is the desire to own something and the ability to pay for it. The term _________ signifies the ability or the willingness to buy a particular commodity at a given point of time .

a. Demand
b. Discretionary spending
c. Market system
d. Market dominance

13. In economics, the _________ can be defined as the graph depicting the relationship between the price of a certain commodity, and the amount of it that consumers are willing and able to purchase at that given price. It is a graphic representation of a demand schedule The _________ for all consumers together follows from the _________ of every individual consumer: the individual demands at each price are added together.

_________s are used to estimate behaviors in competitive markets, and are often combined with supply curves to estimate the equilibrium price (the price at which sellers together are willing to sell the same amount as buyers together are willing to buy, also known as market clearing price) and the equilibrium quantity (the amount of that good or service that will be produced and bought without surplus/excess supply or shortage/excess demand) of that market.

a. Demand curve
b. 6-3-5 Brainwriting
c. Power III
d. 180SearchAssistant

14. According to the American Marketing Association, _________ is the marketing of products that are presumed to be environmentally safe. Thus _________ incorporates a broad range of activities, including product modification, changes to the production process, packaging changes, as well as modifying advertising. Yet defining _________ is not a simple task where several meanings intersect and contradict each other; an example of this will be the existence of varying social, environmental and retail definitions attached to this term.

a. Customer Interaction Tracker
b. Green marketing
c. Commercialization
d. Value proposition

15. _________ is one of the four Ps of the marketing mix. The other three aspects are product, promotion, and place. It is also a key variable in microeconomic price allocation theory.

a. Price
b. Pricing
c. Competitor indexing
d. Relationship based pricing

16. A _________ is a commercial building for storage of goods. _________s are used by manufacturers, importers, exporters, wholesalers, transport businesses, customs, etc. They are usually large plain buildings in industrial areas of cities and towns.

a. Power III
b. 180SearchAssistant
c. Warehouse
d. 6-3-5 Brainwriting

17. The _________ is a professional association for marketers. As of 2008 it had approximately 40,000 members. There are collegiate chapters on 250 campuses.

a. American Marketing Association
b. ADTECH
c. ACNielsen
d. AMAX

18. _________ is a form of government regulation which protects the interests of consumers. For example, a government may require businesses to disclose detailed information about products--particularly in areas where safety or public health is an issue, such as food. _________ is linked to the idea of consumer rights (that consumers have various rights as consumers), and to the formation of consumer organizations which help consumers make better choices in the marketplace.

a. Trademark dilution
b. Federal Bureau of Investigation
c. Sound trademark
d. Consumer protection

19. Combining Existing _________ Sources with New Primary Data Sources

Imagine that we could get hold of a good collection of surveys taken in earlier years, such as detailed studies about changes going on in this phase and hopefully additional studies in the years to come. Analyzing this data base over time could give us a good picture of what changes actually have taken place in the orientation of the population and of the extent to which new technical concepts did have an impact on subgroups of the population. Furthermore, data archives can help to prepare studies on change over time by monitoring what questions have been asked in earlier years and alerting principal investigators to important questions which should be repeated in planned research projects.

a. 180SearchAssistant
b. 6-3-5 Brainwriting
c. Power III
d. Secondary data

20. The United States _________ is the government agency that is responsible for the United States Census. It also gathers other national demographic and economic data.

a. 6-3-5 Brainwriting
b. 180SearchAssistant
c. Power III
d. Census Bureau

21. _________ is a term for unprocessed data, it is also known as primary data. It is a relative term _________ can be input to a computer program or used in manual analysis procedures such as gathering statistics from a survey.

a. Shoppers Food ' Pharmacy
b. Chief marketing officer
c. Product manager
d. Raw data

22. A _________ is a type of website, usually maintained by an individual with regular entries of commentary, descriptions of events, or other material such as graphics or video. Entries are commonly displayed in reverse-chronological order. '_________' can also be used as a verb, meaning to maintain or add content to a _________.

a. Power III
b. 180SearchAssistant
c. 6-3-5 Brainwriting
d. Blog

23. _________ is a type of research conducted because a problem has not been clearly defined. _________ helps determine the best research design, data collection method and selection of subjects. Given its fundamental nature, _________ often concludes that a perceived problem does not actually exist.

a. ACNielsen
b. Exploratory research
c. Intent scale translation
d. IDDEA

24. _________ is either an activity of a living being (such as a human), consisting of receiving knowledge of the outside world through the senses, or the recording of data using scientific instruments. The term may also refer to any datum collected during this activity.

The scientific method requires _________s of nature to formulate and test hypotheses.

a. ADTECH
b. Observation
c. AMAX
d. ACNielsen

25. A _________ is a form of qualitative research in which a group of people are asked about their attitude towards a product, service, concept, advertisement, idea, or packaging. Questions are asked in an interactive group setting where participants are free to talk with other group members.

Ernest Dichter originated the idea of having a 'group therapy' for products and this process is what became known as a _________.

a. Focus group
b. Cross tabulation
c. Logit analysis
d. Marketing research process

26. _________ is one of the four growth strategies of the Product-Market Growth Matrix defined by Ansoff. _________ occurs when a company enters/penetrates a market with current products. The best way to achieve this is by gaining competitors' customers (part of their market share.)

a. Marketization
b. Market penetration
c. Pasar pagi
d. Horizontal market

27. A _________ is a research instrument consisting of a series of questions and other prompts for the purpose of gathering information from respondents. Although they are often designed for statistical analysis of the responses, this is not always the case. The _________ was invented by Sir Francis Galton.

a. Market research
b. Questionnaire
c. Mystery shopping
d. Mystery shoppers

28. _________ a research method involving the use of questionnaires and/or statistical surveys to gather data about people and their thoughts and behaviours.

a. Z-test
b. Survey research
c. Control chart
d. T-test

29. In economics ' business, specifically cost accounting, the _________ is the point at which cost or expenses and revenue are equal: there is no net loss or gain, and one has 'broken even'. A profit or a loss has not been made, although opportunity costs have been paid, and capital has received the risk-adjusted, expected return.

For example, if the business sells less than 200 tables each month, it will make a loss, if it sells more, it will be a profit.

a. Total revenue
b. 180SearchAssistant
c. Power III
d. Break-even point

30. _________ is a process of gathering, modeling, and transforming data with the goal of highlighting useful information, suggesting conclusions, and supporting decision making. _________ has multiple facets and approaches, encompassing diverse techniques under a variety of names, in different business, science, and social science domains.

Data mining is a particular _________ technique that focuses on modeling and knowledge discovery for predictive rather than purely descriptive purposes.

a. Power III
b. 6-3-5 Brainwriting
c. 180SearchAssistant
d. Data Analysis

31. _________ is systematic determination of merit, worth, and significance of something or someone using criteria against a set of standards. _________ often is used to characterize and appraise subjects of interest in a wide range of human enterprises, including the arts, criminal justice, foundations and non-profit organizations, government, health care, and other human services.

Depending on the topic of interest, there are professional groups which look to the quality and rigor of the _________ process.

a. ADTECH
b. AMAX
c. ACNielsen
d. Evaluation

32. An _________ is a series of advertisement messages that share a single idea and theme which make up an integrated marketing communication (IMC.) _________s appear in different media across a specific time frame.

The critical part of making an _________ is determining a campaign theme, as it sets the tone for the individual advertisements and other forms of marketing communications that will be used.

a. ACNielsen
b. ADTECH
c. AMAX
d. Advertising campaign

33. An _________ is the manufacturing of a good or service within a category. Although _________ is a broad term for any kind of economic production, in economics and urban planning _________ is a synonym for the secondary sector, which is a type of economic activity involved in the manufacturing of raw materials into goods and products.

There are four key industrial economic sectors: the primary sector, largely raw material extraction industries such as mining and farming; the secondary sector, involving refining, construction, and manufacturing; the tertiary sector, which deals with services (such as law and medicine) and distribution of manufactured goods; and the quaternary sector, a relatively new type of knowledge _________ focusing on technological research, design and development such as computer programming, and biochemistry.

a. ACNielsen
b. AMAX
c. Industry
d. ADTECH

34. The _________ or _________ is used by business and government to classify and measure economic activity in Canada, Mexico and the United States. It has largely replaced the older Standard Industrial Classification system; however, certain government departments and agencies, such as the U.S. Securities and Exchange Commission (SEC), still use the SIC codes.

The _________ numbering system is a six-digit code.

a. 180SearchAssistant
b. Power III
c. 6-3-5 Brainwriting
d. North American Industry Classification System

1. A _________ is a collection of symbols, experiences and associations connected with a product, a service, a person or any other artifact or entity.

_________s have become increasingly important components of culture and the economy, now being described as 'cultural accessories and personal philosophies'.

Some people distinguish the psychological aspect of a _________ from the experiential aspect.

a. Brandable software
b. Store brand
c. Brand equity
d. Brand

2. In business and engineering, new _________ is the term used to describe the complete process of bringing a new product or service to market. There are two parallel paths involved in the Nproduct development process: one involves the idea generation, product design, and detail engineering; the other involves market research and marketing analysis. Companies typically see new _________ as the first stage in generating and commercializing new products within the overall strategic process of product life cycle management used to maintain or grow their market share.

a. New product screening
b. Product development
c. New product development
d. Specification tree

3. _________ is a rivalry between individuals, groups, nations for territory, a niche, or allocation of resources. It arises whenever two or more parties strive for a goal which cannot be shared. _________ occurs naturally between living organisms which co-exist in the same environment.

a. Competition
b. Non-price competition
c. Price fixing
d. Price competition

4. _________ can be regarded as an outcome of mental processes (cognitive process) leading to the selection of a course of action among several alternatives. Every _________ process produces a final choice. The output can be an action or an opinion of choice.

a. Decision making
b. 6-3-5 Brainwriting
c. Power III
d. 180SearchAssistant

5. _________ is defined by the American _________ Association as the activity, set of institutions, and processes for creating, communicating, delivering, and exchanging offerings that have value for customers, clients, partners, and society at large. The term developed from the original meaning which referred literally to going to market, as in shopping, or going to a market to sell goods or services.

_________ practice tends to be seen as a creative industry, which includes advertising, distribution and selling.

a. Customer acquisition management
b. Marketing
c. Marketing myopia
d. Product naming

6. The _________ is generally accepted as the use and specification of the four p's describing the strategic position of a product in the marketplace. One version of the origins of the _________ starts in 1948 when James Culliton said that a marketing decision should be a result of something similar to a recipe. This version continued in 1953 when Neil Borden, in his American Marketing Association presidential address, took the recipe idea one step further and coined the term 'Marketing-Mix'.

a. Marketing mix
b. Power III
c. 6-3-5 Brainwriting
d. 180SearchAssistant

7. _________ deals with the first of the '4P''s of marketing, which are Product, Pricing, Place, and Promotion. _________, as opposed to product management, deals with more outbound marketing tasks. For example, product management deals with the nuts and bolts of product development within a firm, whereas _________ deals with marketing the product to prospects, customers, and others.

a. Crisis management
b. Corporate transparency
c. Reverse hierarchy
d. Product Marketing

8. There are many important decisions about product and service development and marketing. In the process of product development and marketing we should focus on strategic decisions about product attributes, product branding, product packaging, product labeling and product support services. But product strategy also calls for building a _________.

a. Pinstorm
b. Macromarketing
c. Technology acceptance model
d. Product line

9. A personal and cultural _________ is a relative ethic _________, an assumption upon which implementation can be extrapolated. A _________ system is a set of consistent _________s and measures that is soo not true. A principle _________ is a foundation upon which other _________s and measures of integrity are based.

a. Perceptual maps
b. Package-on-Package
c. Supreme Court of the United States
d. Value

10. _________, in marketing, consists of a consumer's commitment to repurchase the brand and can be demonstrated by repeated buying of a product or service or other positive behaviors such as word of mouth advocacy. True _________ implies that the consumer is willing, at least on occasion, to put aside their own desires in the interest of the brand. _________ has been proclaimed by some to be the ultimate goal of marketing.

a. Brand awareness
b. Trade Symbols
c. Brand loyalty
d. Brand implementation

11. In economics, business, retail, and accounting, a _________ is the value of money that has been used up to produce something, and hence is not available for use anymore. In economics, a _________ is an alternative that is given up as a result of a decision. In business, the _________ may be one of acquisition, in which case the amount of money expended to acquire it is counted as _________.

a. Variable cost
b. Fixed costs
c. Transaction cost
d. Cost

12. _________ in economics and business is the result of an exchange and from that trade we assign a numerical monetary value to a good, service or asset. If I trade 4 apples for an orange, the _________ of an orange is 4 - apples. Inversely, the _________ of an apple is 1/4 oranges.

a. Contribution margin-based pricing
b. Discounts and allowances
c. Price
d. Pricing

13. _________ is one of the four Ps of the marketing mix. The other three aspects are product, promotion, and place. It is also a key variable in microeconomic price allocation theory.

a. Competitor indexing
b. Price
c. Pricing
d. Relationship based pricing

14. _________ refers to the marketing effects or outcomes that accrue to a product with its brand name compared with those that would accrue if the same product did not have the brand name . And, at the root of these marketing effects is consumers' knowledge. In other words, consumers' knowledge about a brand makes manufacturers/advertisers respond differently or adopt appropriately adapt measures for the marketing of the brand .

a. Brand aversion
b. Brand image
c. Product extension
d. Brand equity

15. _________ is the price at which an asset would trade in a competitive Walrasian auction setting. _________ is often used interchangeably with open _________, fair value or fair _________, although these terms have distinct definitions in different standards, and may differ in some circumstances.

International Valuation Standards defines _________ as 'the estimated amount for which a property should exchange on the date of valuation between a willing buyer and a willing seller in an arm's-length transaction after proper marketing wherein the parties had each acted knowledgeably, prudently, and without compulsion.'

_________ is a concept distinct from market price, which is 'the price at which one can transact', while _________ is 'the true underlying value' according to theoretical standards.

a. Restructuring
b. Power III
c. 180SearchAssistant
d. Market value

16. _________ is a marketing concept that refers to a consumer knowing of a brand's existence; at aggregate (brand) level it refers to the proportion of consumers who know of the brand.

_________ can be measured by showing a consumer the brand and asking whether or not they knew of it beforehand. However, in common market research practice a variety of recognition and recall measures of _________ are employed all of which test the brand name's association to a product category cue, this came about because most market research in the 20th Century was conducted by post or telephone, actually showing the brand to consumers usually required more expensive face-to-face interviews (until web-based interviews became possible.)

a. Brand equity
b. Brand orientation
c. Fitting Group
d. Brand awareness

17. _________ consists of the processes a company uses to track and organize its contacts with its current and prospective customers. _________ software is used to support these processes; information about customers and customer interactions can be entered, stored and accessed by employees in different company departments. Typical _________ goals are to improve services provided to customers, and to use customer contact information for targeted marketing.

a. Customer relationship management
b. Commercialization
c. Product bundling
d. Demand generation

18. Customer _________ consists of the processes a company uses to track and organize its contacts with its current and prospective customers. CRelationship management software is used to support these processes; information about customers and customer interactions can be entered, stored and accessed by employees in different company departments. Typical CRelationship management goals are to improve services provided to customers, and to use customer contact information for targeted marketing.

a. Green marketing
b. Marketing
c. Product bundling
d. Relationship management

19. The brand name of a product that is distributed nationally under a brand name owned by the producer or distributor, as opposed to local brands (products distributed only in some areas of the country), and private label brands (products that carry the brand of the retailer rather than the producer.)

_________s must compete with local and private brands._________s are produced by ,widely distuted by, and carry the name of the manufacturer.

- Local brands may appeal to those consumers who favor small, local producers over large national or global producers, and may be willing to pay a premium to 'buy local'

- The private label producer can offer lower prices because they avoid the cost of marketing and advertising to create and protect the brand. In North America, large retailers such as Loblaws, Walgreen and Wal-Mart all offer private label products.

a. National brand
b. Market intelligence
c. Specialty catalogs
d. Line extension

20. _________ is the state or fact of exclusive rights and control over property, which may be an object, land/real estate, or some other kind of property (like government-granted monopolies collectively referred to as intellectual property.) It is embodied in an _________ right also referred to as title.

_________ is the key building block in the development of the capitalist socio-economic system.

a. ACNielsen
b. AMAX
c. Ownership
d. ADTECH

21. _________s (house brands in the United States, own brands in the UK, and home brands in Australia) are brands which are specific to a retail store or store chain. The retailer can manufacture goods under its own label, re-brand private label goods, or outsource manufacture of _________ items to multiple third parties - often the same manufacturers that produce brand label goods. _________ goods are generally cheaper than national brand goods because the retailer can optimize the production to suit consumer demand and reduce advertising costs.

a. Brand ambassador
b. Brand strength analysis
c. Brand loyalty
d. Store brand

22. _________ or brand stretching is a marketing strategy in which a firm marketing a product with a well-developed image uses the same brand name in a different product category. Organizations use this strategy to increase and leverage brand equity (definition: the net worth and long-term sustainability just from the renowned name.) An example of a _________ is Jello-gelatin creating Jello pudding pops.

a. Web 2.0
b. Brand extension
c. Brand awareness
d. Brand orientation

23. _________ is a trademark law concept permitting the owner of a famous trademark to forbid others from using that mark in a way that would lessen its uniqueness. In most cases, _________ involves an unauthorized use of another's trademark on products that do not compete with, and have little connection with, those of the trademark owner. For example, a famous trademark used by one company to refer to hair care products might be diluted if another company began using a similar mark to refer to breakfast cereals or spark plugs.

a. Trespass to land
b. Trademark attorney
c. Federal Bureau of Investigation
d. Trademark dilution

24. _________ is the process of creating and managing contracts between the owner of a brand and a company or individual who wants to use the brand in association with a product, for an agreed period of time, within an agreed territory. Licensing is used by brand owners to extend a trademark or character onto products of a completely different nature.

_________ a is well-established business, both in the area of patents and trademarks.

a. Brand loyalty
b. Brand culture
c. Brand licensing
d. Brand strength analysis

25. The verb _________ or grant _________ means to give permission. The noun _________ refers to that permission as well as to the document memorializing that permission. _________ may be granted by a party to another party as an element of an agreement between those parties.

a. Power III
b. 6-3-5 Brainwriting
c. 180SearchAssistant
d. License

26. _________ is the process by which a product or service developed with one brand, company or product line affiliation is marketed or distributed with a different identity. This may involve radical changes to the brand's logo, brand name, image, marketing strategy, and advertising themes. These changes are typically aimed at the repositioning of the brand/company, usually in an attempt to distance itself from certain negative connotations of the previous branding, or to move the brand upmarket.

a. Foreign branding
b. Nation branding
c. Faith branding
d. Rebranding

27. _________ is a broad label that refers to any individuals or households that use goods and services generated within the economy. The concept of a _________ is used in different contexts, so that the usage and significance of the term may vary.

A _________ is a person who uses any product or service.

a. Power III
b. 180SearchAssistant
c. 6-3-5 Brainwriting
d. Consumer

28. The _________ is a US law that applies to labels on many consumer products. It requires the label to state:

- The identity of the product;
- The name and place of business of the manufacturer, packer, or distributor; and
- The net quantity of contents.

The contents statement must include both metric and U.S. customary units.

Passed under Lyndon B. Johnson in 1966, the law first took effect on July 1, 1967. The metric labeling requirement was added in 1992 and took effect on February 14, 1994.

a. Fair Packaging and Labeling Act
b. 180SearchAssistant
c. 6-3-5 Brainwriting
d. Power III

29. _________ is a scientific discipline describing handling, preparation, and storage of food in ways that prevent foodborne illness. This includes a number of routines that should be followed to avoid potentially severe health hazards. Food can transmit disease from person to person as well as serve as a growth medium for bacteria that can cause food poisoning.

a. Shelf life
b. Power III
c. 180SearchAssistant
d. Food Safety

30. _________ is an advertisement in which a particular product specifically mentions a competitor by name for the express purpose of showing why the competitor is inferior to the product naming it.

This should not be confused with parody advertisements, where a fictional product is being advertised for the purpose of poking fun at the particular advertisement, nor should it be confused with the use of a coined brand name for the purpose of comparing the product without actually naming an actual competitor. ('Wikipedia tastes better and is less filling than the Encyclopedia Galactica.')

In the 1980s, during what has been referred to as the cola wars, soft-drink manufacturer Pepsi ran a series of advertisements where people, caught on hidden camera, in a blind taste test, chose Pepsi over rival Coca-Cola.

a. GL-70
b. Cost per conversion
c. Heavy-up
d. Comparative advertising

31. _________ is a form of government regulation which protects the interests of consumers. For example, a government may require businesses to disclose detailed information about products--particularly in areas where safety or public health is an issue, such as food. _________ is linked to the idea of consumer rights (that consumers have various rights as consumers), and to the formation of consumer organizations which help consumers make better choices in the marketplace.

a. Sound trademark
b. Federal Bureau of Investigation
c. Consumer protection
d. Trademark dilution

32. An _________ is a situation that will often involve an apparent conflict between moral imperatives, in which to obey one would result in transgressing another. This is also called an ethical paradox since in moral philosophy, paradox plays a central role in ethics debates. For instance, an ethical admonition to 'love thy neighbour as thy self' is not always just in contrast with, but sometimes in contradiction to an armed neighbour actively trying to kill you: if he or she succeeds, you will not be able to love him or her.

a. AMAX
b. ACNielsen
c. ADTECH
d. Ethical dilemma

33. _________ is a form of communication that typically attempts to persuade potential customers to purchase or to consume more of a particular brand of product or service. 'While now central to the contemporary global economy and the reproduction of global production networks, it is only quite recently that _________ has been more than a marginal influence on patterns of sales and production. The formation of modern _________ was intimately bound up with the emergence of new forms of monopoly capitalism around the end of the 19th and beginning of the 20th century as one element in corporate strategies to create, organize and where possible control markets, especially for mass produced consumer goods.

a. ACNielsen
b. Advertising
c. AMAX
d. ADTECH

1. In business and engineering, new _________ is the term used to describe the complete process of bringing a new product or service to market. There are two parallel paths involved in the Nproduct development process: one involves the idea generation, product design, and detail engineering; the other involves market research and marketing analysis. Companies typically see new _________ as the first stage in generating and commercializing new products within the overall strategic process of product life cycle management used to maintain or grow their market share.

a. New product screening
b. New product development
c. Specification tree
d. Product development

2. A personal and cultural _________ is a relative ethic _________, an assumption upon which implementation can be extrapolated. A _________ system is a set of consistent _________s and measures that is soo not true. A principle _________ is a foundation upon which other _________s and measures of integrity are based.

a. Value
b. Perceptual maps
c. Supreme Court of the United States
d. Package-on-Package

3. A _________ is a collection of symbols, experiences and associations connected with a product, a service, a person or any other artifact or entity.

_________s have become increasingly important components of culture and the economy, now being described as 'cultural accessories and personal philosophies'.

Some people distinguish the psychological aspect of a _________ from the experiential aspect.

a. Store brand
b. Brand
c. Brand equity
d. Brandable software

4. _________ is the process by which a new idea or new product is accepted by the market. The rate of _________ is the speed that the new idea spreads from one consumer to the next. Adoption is similar to _________ except that it deals with the psychological processes an individual goes through, rather than an aggregate market process.

a. Diffusion
b. Market development
c. Perceptual maps
d. Kano model

5. _________ is a theory of how, why, and at what rate new ideas and technology spread through cultures. Everett Rogers introduced it in his 1962 book, _________s, writing that 'Diffusion is the process by which an innovation is communicated through certain channels over time among the members of a social system.' The adoption curve becomes an s-curve when cumulative adoption is used.

Rogers theorized that innovations would spread through a community in an S curve, as the early adopters select the innovation (which may be a technology) first, followed by the majority, until a technology or innovation has reached its saturation point in a community.

According to Rogers, diffusion research centers on the conditions which increase or decrease the likelihood that a new idea, product, or practice will be adopted by members of a given culture.

a. 6-3-5 Brainwriting
b. 180SearchAssistant
c. Power III
d. Diffusion of innovation

6. The phrase _________, according to the Organization for Economic Co-operation and Development, refers to 'creative work undertaken on a systematic basis in order to increase the stock of knowledge, including knowledge of man, culture and society, and the use of this stock of knowledge to devise new applications [sic]' Though it is questionable that an organization is needed for this definition, as it is quite obvious that _________ refers to the _________ of something.

New product design and development is more often than not a crucial factor in the survival of a company. In an industry that is fast changing, firms must continually revise their design and range of products.

a. Power III
b. 180SearchAssistant
c. 6-3-5 Brainwriting
d. Research and development

7. _________ is a group creativity technique designed to generate a large number of ideas for the solution of a problem. The method was first popularized in the late 1930s by Alex Faickney Osborn in a book called Applied Imagination. Osborn proposed that groups could double their creative output with _________.

a. Albert Einstein
b. African Americans
c. AStore
d. Brainstorming

8. _________ is a rivalry between individuals, groups, nations for territory, a niche, or allocation of resources. It arises whenever two or more parties strive for a goal which cannot be shared. _________ occurs naturally between living organisms which co-exist in the same environment.

a. Competition
b. Price fixing
c. Non-price competition
d. Price competition

9. The verb _________ or grant _________ means to give permission. The noun _________ refers to that permission as well as to the document memorializing that permission. _________ may be granted by a party to another party as an element of an agreement between those parties.

a. Power III
b. 180SearchAssistant
c. License
d. 6-3-5 Brainwriting

10. _________ is the process of using quantitative methods and qualitative methods to evaluate consumer response to a product idea prior to the introduction of a product to the market. It can also be used to generate communication designed to alter consumer attitudes toward existing products. These methods involve the evaluation by consumers of product concepts having certain rational benefits, such as 'a detergent that removes stains but is gentle on fabrics,' or non-rational benefits, such as 'a shampoo that lets you be yourself.' Such methods are commonly referred to as _________ and have been performed using field surveys, personal interviews and focus groups, in combination with various quantitative methods, to generate and evaluate product concepts.

a. Cross tabulation
b. Logit analysis
c. Market analysis
d. Concept testing

11. _________ is a term developed by Eric von Hippel in 1986. His definition for _________ is:

1. _________s face needs that will be general in a marketplace - but face them months or years before the bulk of that marketplace encounters them, and
2. _________s are positioned to benefit significantly by obtaining a solution to those needs.

In other words: _________s are users of a product that currently experience needs still unknown to the public and who also benefit greatly if they obtain a solution to these needs.

The _________ Method is a market research tool that may be used by companies and / or individuals seeking to develop breakthrough products. _________ methodology was originally developed by Dr. Eric von Hippel of the Massachusetts Institute of Technology (MIT) and first described in the July 1986 issue of the Journal of Management Science.

a. 180SearchAssistant
b. Power III
c. Lead user
d. 6-3-5 Brainwriting

12. In economics, _________ is the desire to own something and the ability to pay for it. The term _________ signifies the ability or the willingness to buy a particular commodity at a given point of time .

.

a. Market dominance
b. Discretionary spending
c. Demand
d. Market system

13. In economics, the _________ can be defined as the graph depicting the relationship between the price of a certain commodity, and the amount of it that consumers are willing and able to purchase at that given price. It is a graphic representation of a demand schedule The _________ for all consumers together follows from the _________ of every individual consumer: the individual demands at each price are added together.

_________s are used to estimate behaviors in competitive markets, and are often combined with supply curves to estimate the equilibrium price (the price at which sellers together are willing to sell the same amount as buyers together are willing to buy, also known as market clearing price) and the equilibrium quantity (the amount of that good or service that will be produced and bought without surplus/excess supply or shortage/excess demand) of that market.

a. Demand curve
b. Power III
c. 180SearchAssistant
d. 6-3-5 Brainwriting

14. _________ is one of the four Ps of the marketing mix. The other three aspects are product, promotion, and place. It is also a key variable in microeconomic price allocation theory.

a. Competitor indexing
b. Relationship based pricing
c. Price
d. Pricing

15. An _________ is a situation that will often involve an apparent conflict between moral imperatives, in which to obey one would result in transgressing another. This is also called an ethical paradox since in moral philosophy, paradox plays a central role in ethics debates. For instance, an ethical admonition to 'love thy neighbour as thy self' is not always just in contrast with, but sometimes in contradiction to an armed neighbour actively trying to kill you: if he or she succeeds, you will not be able to love him or her.

a. ADTECH
b. AMAX
c. ACNielsen
d. Ethical dilemma

16. _________ is a form of communication that typically attempts to persuade potential customers to purchase or to consume more of a particular brand of product or service. 'While now central to the contemporary global economy and the reproduction of global production networks, it is only quite recently that _________ has been more than a marginal influence on patterns of sales and production. The formation of modern _________ was intimately bound up with the emergence of new forms of monopoly capitalism around the end of the 19th and beginning of the 20th century as one element in corporate strategies to create, organize and where possible control markets, especially for mass produced consumer goods.

a. ACNielsen
b. Advertising
c. AMAX
d. ADTECH

17. _________ can be defined as the idea generation, concept development, testing and manufacturing or implementation of a physical object or service. _________ers conceptualize and evaluate ideas, making them tangible through products in a more systematic approach. The role of a _________er encompasses many characteristics of the marketing manager, product manager, industrial designer and design engineer.

a. AStore
b. Albert Einstein
c. African Americans
d. Product design

18. Proof-of-Principle _________ This type of _________ is used to test some aspect of the intended design without attempting to exactly simulate the visual appearance, choice of materials or intended manufacturing process. Such _________s can be used to 'prove' out a potential design approach such as range of motion, mechanics, sensors, architecture, etc.

a. 6-3-5 Brainwriting
b. Power III
c. Prototype
d. 180SearchAssistant

19. A _________, in the field of business and marketing, is a geographic region or demographic group used to gauge the viability of a product or service in the mass market prior to a wide scale roll-out. The criteria used to judge the acceptability of a _________ region or group include:

1. a population that is demographically similar to the proposed target market; and
2. relative isolation from densely populated media markets so that advertising to the test audience can be efficient and economical.

The _________ ideally aims to duplicate 'everything' - promotion and distribution as well as `product' - on a smaller scale. The technique replicates, typically in one area, what is planned to occur in a national launch; and the results are very carefully monitored, so that they can be extrapolated to projected national results. The `area' may be any one of the following:

- Television area
- Test town
- Residential neighborhood
- Test site

A number of decisions have to be taken about any _________:

- Which _________?
- What is to be tested?
- How long a test?
- What are the success criteria?

The simple go or no-go decision, together with the related reduction of risk, is normally the main justification for the expense of _________s. At the same time, however, such _________s can be used to test specific elements of a new product's marketing mix; possibly the version of the product itself, the promotional message and media spend, the distribution channels and the price.

a. Preadolescence
b. 180SearchAssistant
c. Test market
d. Power III

20. _________ is defined by the American _________ Association as the activity, set of institutions, and processes for creating, communicating, delivering, and exchanging offerings that have value for customers, clients, partners, and society at large. The term developed from the original meaning which referred literally to going to market, as in shopping, or going to a market to sell goods or services.

_________ practice tends to be seen as a creative industry, which includes advertising, distribution and selling.

a. Marketing
b. Customer acquisition management
c. Product naming
d. Marketing myopia

21. _________ , according to The American Marketing Association, is 'a planning process designed to assure that all brand contacts received by a customer or prospect for a product, service, or organization are relevant to that person and consistent over time.' (Marketing Power Dictionary)

_________ is a term used to describe a holistic approach to marketing. It aims to ensure consistency of message and the complementary use of media. The concept includes online and offline marketing channels.

a. ADTECH
b. AMAX
c. ACNielsen
d. Integrated marketing communications

22. _________ involves disseminating information about a product, product line, brand, or company. It is one of the four key aspects of the marketing mix. (The other three elements are product marketing, pricing, and distribution). P>_________ is generally sub-divided into two parts:

- Above the line _________: Promotion in the media (e.g. TV, radio, newspapers, Internet and Mobile Phones) in which the advertiser pays an advertising agency to place the ad
- Below the line _________: All other _________. Much of this is intended to be subtle enough for the consumer to be unaware that _________ is taking place. E.g. sponsorship, product placement, endorsements, sales _________, merchandising, direct mail, personal selling, public relations, trade shows

a. Bottling lines
b. Davie Brown Index
c. Cashmere Agency
d. Promotion

23. A _________ or logistics network is the system of organizations, people, technology, activities, information and resources involved in moving a product or service from supplier to customer. _________ activities transform natural resources, raw materials and components into a finished product that is delivered to the end customer. In sophisticated _________ systems, used products may re-enter the _________ at any point where residual value is recyclable.

a. Demand chain management
b. Supply chain
c. Purchasing
d. Supply chain network

24. _________ is a broad label that refers to any individuals or households that use goods and services generated within the economy. The concept of a _________ is used in different contexts, so that the usage and significance of the term may vary.

A _________ is a person who uses any product or service.

a. 180SearchAssistant
b. Power III
c. Consumer
d. 6-3-5 Brainwriting

25. _________ is the study of when, why, how, where and what people do or do not buy products. It blends elements from psychology, sociology,social psychology, anthropology and economics. It attempts to understand the buyer decision making process, both individually and in groups. It studies characteristics of individual consumers such as demographics and behavioural variables in an attempt to understand people's wants. It also tries to assess influences on the consumer from groups such as family, friends, reference groups, and society in general.

a. Communal marketing
b. Multidimensional scaling
c. Consumer confidence
d. Consumer behavior

26. _________ refers to messages and related media used to communicate with a market. Those who practice advertising, branding, direct marketing, graphic design, marketing, packaging, promotion, publicity, sponsorship, public relations, sales, sales promotion and online marketing are termed marketing communicators, _________ managers, or more briefly as marcom managers.

a. Merchandising
b. Sales promotion
c. Merchandise
d. Marketing communication

27. _________ is systematic determination of merit, worth, and significance of something or someone using criteria against a set of standards. _________ often is used to characterize and appraise subjects of interest in a wide range of human enterprises, including the arts, criminal justice, foundations and non-profit organizations, government, health care, and other human services.

Depending on the topic of interest, there are professional groups which look to the quality and rigor of the _________ process.

a. ADTECH
b. Evaluation
c. AMAX
d. ACNielsen

28. _________ Management is the succession of strategies used by management as a product goes through its _________. The conditions in which a product is sold changes over time and must be managed as it moves through its succession of stages.

The _________ goes through many phases, involves many professional disciplines, and requires many skills, tools and processes.

a. Supplier diversity
b. Customer satisfaction
c. Product life cycle
d. Chain stores

29. An _________ is a series of advertisement messages that share a single idea and theme which make up an integrated marketing communication (IMC.) _________s appear in different media across a specific time frame.

The critical part of making an _________ is determining a campaign theme, as it sets the tone for the individual advertisements and other forms of marketing communications that will be used.

a. Advertising campaign
b. AMAX
c. ACNielsen
d. ADTECH

30. A _________ is a subgroup of people or organizations sharing one or more characteristics that cause them to have similar product and/or service needs. A true _________ meets all of the following criteria: it is distinct from other segments (different segments have different needs), it is homogeneous within the segment (exhibits common needs); it responds similarly to a market stimulus, and it can be reached by a market intervention. The term is also used when consumers with identical product and/or service needs are divided up into groups so they can be charged different amounts.

a. Customer insight
b. Commercial planning
c. Production orientation
d. Market segment

31. In marketing, _________ has come to mean the process by which marketers try to create an image or identity in the minds of their target market for its product, brand, or organization. It is the 'relative competitive comparison' their product occupies in a given market as perceived by the target market.

Re-_________ involves changing the identity of a product, relative to the identity of competing products, in the collective minds of the target market.

a. Moratorium
b. GE matrix
c. Positioning
d. Containerization

1. _________ is the provision of service to customers before, during and after a purchase.

According to Turban et al., '_________ is a series of activities designed to enhance the level of customer satisfaction - that is, the feeling that a product or service has met the customer expectation.'

Its importance varies by product, industry and customer.

a. Customer service
b. Facing
c. COPC Inc.
d. Customer experience

2. _________ is an advertisement in which a particular product specifically mentions a competitor by name for the express purpose of showing why the competitor is inferior to the product naming it.

This should not be confused with parody advertisements, where a fictional product is being advertised for the purpose of poking fun at the particular advertisement, nor should it be confused with the use of a coined brand name for the purpose of comparing the product without actually naming an actual competitor. ('Wikipedia tastes better and is less filling than the Encyclopedia Galactica.')

In the 1980s, during what has been referred to as the cola wars, soft-drink manufacturer Pepsi ran a series of advertisements where people, caught on hidden camera, in a blind taste test, chose Pepsi over rival Coca-Cola.

a. Comparative advertising
b. Cost per conversion
c. Heavy-up
d. GL-70

3. In business and engineering, new _________ is the term used to describe the complete process of bringing a new product or service to market. There are two parallel paths involved in the Nproduct development process: one involves the idea generation, product design, and detail engineering; the other involves market research and marketing analysis. Companies typically see new _________ as the first stage in generating and commercializing new products within the overall strategic process of product life cycle management used to maintain or grow their market share.

a. Product development
b. New product development
c. New product screening
d. Specification tree

4. _________ is defined by the American _________ Association as the activity, set of institutions, and processes for creating, communicating, delivering, and exchanging offerings that have value for customers, clients, partners, and society at large. The term developed from the original meaning which referred literally to going to market, as in shopping, or going to a market to sell goods or services.

_________ practice tends to be seen as a creative industry, which includes advertising, distribution and selling.

a. Customer acquisition management
b. Marketing myopia
c. Product naming
d. Marketing

5. _________ deals with the first of the '4P''s of marketing, which are Product, Pricing, Place, and Promotion. _________, as opposed to product management, deals with more outbound marketing tasks. For example, product management deals with the nuts and bolts of product development within a firm, whereas _________ deals with marketing the product to prospects, customers, and others.

a. Crisis management
b. Reverse hierarchy
c. Corporate transparency
d. Product marketing

6. _________ is marketing based on relationship and value. It may be used to market a service or a product.

Marketing a service-base business is different from marketing a goods-base business.

a. Power III
b. 6-3-5 Brainwriting
c. Services marketing
d. 180SearchAssistant

7. _________ is used in marketing to describe a key quality of services as distinct from goods. _________ is the characteristic that a service has which renders it impossible to divorce the supply or production of the service from its consumption.

Other key characteristics of services include perishability, intangibility and variability.

a. Online focus group
b. Individual branding
c. Engagement
d. Inseparability

8. An _________ is a situation that will often involve an apparent conflict between moral imperatives, in which to obey one would result in transgressing another. This is also called an ethical paradox since in moral philosophy, paradox plays a central role in ethics debates. For instance, an ethical admonition to 'love thy neighbour as thy self' is not always just in contrast with, but sometimes in contradiction to an armed neighbour actively trying to kill you: if he or she succeeds, you will not be able to love him or her.

a. ADTECH
b. AMAX
c. ACNielsen
d. Ethical dilemma

9. _________ is a form of communication that typically attempts to persuade potential customers to purchase or to consume more of a particular brand of product or service. 'While now central to the contemporary global economy and the reproduction of global production networks, it is only quite recently that _________ has been more than a marginal influence on patterns of sales and production. The formation of modern _________ was intimately bound up with the emergence of new forms of monopoly capitalism around the end of the 19th and beginning of the 20th century as one element in corporate strategies to create, organize and where possible control markets, especially for mass produced consumer goods.

a. ACNielsen
b. ADTECH
c. AMAX
d. Advertising

10. _________ is used in marketing to describe the way in which service capacity cannot be stored for sale in the future. It is a key concept of services marketing.

Other key characteristics of services include intangibility, inseparability and variability.

a. Specialty catalogs
b. Demonstrator model
c. National brand
d. Perishability

11. In economics, _________ is the desire to own something and the ability to pay for it. The term _________ signifies the ability or the willingness to buy a particular commodity at a given point of time .

.

a. Market dominance
b. Discretionary spending
c. Market system
d. Demand

12. In economics, the _________ can be defined as the graph depicting the relationship between the price of a certain commodity, and the amount of it that consumers are willing and able to purchase at that given price. It is a graphic representation of a demand schedule The _________ for all consumers together follows from the _________ of every individual consumer: the individual demands at each price are added together.

_________s are used to estimate behaviors in competitive markets, and are often combined with supply curves to estimate the equilibrium price (the price at which sellers together are willing to sell the same amount as buyers together are willing to buy, also known as market clearing price) and the equilibrium quantity (the amount of that good or service that will be produced and bought without surplus/excess supply or shortage/excess demand) of that market.

a. Demand curve
b. 180SearchAssistant
c. Power III
d. 6-3-5 Brainwriting

13. _________ is one of the four Ps of the marketing mix. The other three aspects are product, promotion, and place. It is also a key variable in microeconomic price allocation theory.

a. Competitor indexing
b. Pricing
c. Price
d. Relationship based pricing

14. _________ generally refers to a list of all planned expenses and revenues. It is a plan for saving and spending. A _________ is an important concept in microeconomics, which uses a _________ line to illustrate the trade-offs between two or more goods.

a. 6-3-5 Brainwriting
b. Budget
c. Power III
d. 180SearchAssistant

15. In economics and sociology, an _________ is any factor (financial or non-financial) that enables or motivates a particular course of action, or counts as a reason for preferring one choice to the alternatives. It is an expectation that encourages people to behave in a certain way. Since human beings are purposeful creatures, the study of _________ structures is central to the study of all economic activity (both in terms of individual decision-making and in terms of co-operation and competition within a larger institutional structure.)

a. ACNielsen
b. AMAX
c. Incentive
d. ADTECH

1. _________ in economics and business is the result of an exchange and from that trade we assign a numerical monetary value to a good, service or asset. If I trade 4 apples for an orange, the _________ of an orange is 4 - apples. Inversely, the _________ of an apple is 1/4 oranges.

a. Contribution margin-based pricing
b. Pricing
c. Discounts and allowances
d. Price

2. _________ is one of the four Ps of the marketing mix. The other three aspects are product, promotion, and place. It is also a key variable in microeconomic price allocation theory.

a. Price
b. Competitor indexing
c. Relationship based pricing
d. Pricing

3. In marketing, _________ has come to mean the process by which marketers try to create an image or identity in the minds of their target market for its product, brand, or organization. It is the 'relative competitive comparison' their product occupies in a given market as perceived by the target market.

Re-_________ involves changing the identity of a product, relative to the identity of competing products, in the collective minds of the target market.

a. GE matrix
b. Moratorium
c. Containerization
d. Positioning

4. Competitiveness is a comparative concept of the ability and performance of a firm, sub-sector or country to sell and supply goods and/or services in a given market. Although widely used in economics and business management, the usefulness of the concept, particularly in the context of national competitiveness, is vigorously disputed by economists, such as Paul Krugman .

The term may also be applied to markets, where it is used to refer to the extent to which the market structure may be regarded as perfectly _________.

a. Competitive
b. Customs union
c. Free trade zone
d. Geographical pricing

5. In economics, _________ is the desire to own something and the ability to pay for it. The term _________ signifies the ability or the willingness to buy a particular commodity at a given point of time .

.

a. Market dominance
b. Discretionary spending
c. Market system
d. Demand

6. In economics, the _________ can be defined as the graph depicting the relationship between the price of a certain commodity, and the amount of it that consumers are willing and able to purchase at that given price. It is a graphic representation of a demand schedule The _________ for all consumers together follows from the _________ of every individual consumer: the individual demands at each price are added together.

_________s are used to estimate behaviors in competitive markets, and are often combined with supply curves to estimate the equilibrium price (the price at which sellers together are willing to sell the same amount as buyers together are willing to buy, also known as market clearing price) and the equilibrium quantity (the amount of that good or service that will be produced and bought without surplus/excess supply or shortage/excess demand) of that market.

a. Power III
b. Demand curve
c. 6-3-5 Brainwriting
d. 180SearchAssistant

7. _________ is defined as the measure of responsiveness in the quantity demanded for a commodity as a result of change in price of the same commodity. It is a measure of how consumers react to a change in price. In other words, it is percentage change in quantity demanded as per the percentage change in price of the same commodity.

a. 180SearchAssistant
b. Price elasticity of demand
c. 6-3-5 Brainwriting
d. Power III

8. In economics, _________ is the ratio of the percent change in one variable to the percent change in another variable. It is a tool for measuring the responsiveness of a function to changes in parameters in a relative way. Commonly analyzed are _________ of substitution, price and wealth.

a. ACNielsen
b. Elasticity
c. Intellectual property
d. Opinion leadership

9. Price _________ is defined as the measure of responsiveness in the quantity demanded for a commodity as a result of change in price of the same commodity. It is a measure of how consumers react to a change in price. In other words, it is percentage change in quantity demanded as per the percentage change in price of the same commodity.

a. Elasticity of demand
b. ADTECH
c. AMAX
d. ACNielsen

10. In economics, _________ describes demand that is not very sensitive to a change in price.

a. ACNielsen
b. ADTECH
c. AMAX
d. Inelastic

11. In business and engineering, new _________ is the term used to describe the complete process of bringing a new product or service to market. There are two parallel paths involved in the Nproduct development process: one involves the idea generation, product design, and detail engineering; the other involves market research and marketing analysis. Companies typically see new _________ as the first stage in generating and commercializing new products within the overall strategic process of product life cycle management used to maintain or grow their market share.

a. New product development
b. Specification tree
c. New product screening
d. Product development

12. _________s are used in open sentences. For instance, in the formula x + 1 = 5, x is a _________ which represents an 'unknown' number. _________s are often represented by letters of the Roman alphabet, or those of other alphabets, such as Greek, and use other special symbols.

a. Variable
b. Quantitative
c. Book of business
d. Personalization

13. _________s are expenses that change in proportion to the activity of a business. In other words, _________ is the sum of marginal costs. It can also be considered normal costs.

a. Marginal cost
b. Variable cost
c. Transaction cost
d. Fixed costs

14. In economics, business, retail, and accounting, a _________ is the value of money that has been used up to produce something, and hence is not available for use anymore. In economics, a _________ is an alternative that is given up as a result of a decision. In business, the _________ may be one of acquisition, in which case the amount of money expended to acquire it is counted as _________.

a. Cost
b. Variable cost
c. Transaction cost
d. Fixed costs

15. _________ is a list for goods and materials held available in stock by a business. It is also used for a list of the contents of a household and for a list for testamentary purposes of the possessions of someone who has died. In accounting _________ is considered an asset.

a. ADTECH
b. Inventory
c. Ending Inventory
d. ACNielsen

16. In economics ' business, specifically cost accounting, the _________ is the point at which cost or expenses and revenue are equal: there is no net loss or gain, and one has 'broken even'. A profit or a loss has not been made, although opportunity costs have been paid, and capital has received the risk-adjusted, expected return.

For example, if the business sells less than 200 tables each month, it will make a loss, if it sells more, it will be a profit.

a. Total revenue
b. Power III
c. 180SearchAssistant
d. Break-even point

17. In economics, and cost accounting, _________ describes the total economic cost of production and is made up of variable costs, which vary according to the quantity of a good produced and include inputs such as labor and raw materials, plus fixed costs, which are independent of the quantity of a good produced and include inputs (capital) that cannot be varied in the short term, such as buildings and machinery. _________ in economics includes the total opportunity cost of each factor of production in addition to fixed and variable costs.

The rate at which _________ changes as the amount produced changes is called marginal cost.

a. Household production function
b. Hoarding
c. Total cost
d. Product proliferation

18. The break-even point for a product is the point where total revenue received equals the total costs associated with the sale of the product (TR=TC.) A break-even point is typically calculated in order for businesses to determine if it would be profitable to sell a proposed product, as opposed to attempting to modify an existing product instead so it can be made lucrative. _________ can also be used to analyse the potential profitability of an expenditure in a sales-based business.

In _________, margin of safety is how much output or sales level can fall before a business reaches its break-even point (BEP).

a. Contribution margin-based pricing
b. Break even analysis
c. Price skimming
d. Pay Per Sale

19. _________ can be regarded as an outcome of mental processes (cognitive process) leading to the selection of a course of action among several alternatives. Every _________ process produces a final choice. The output can be an action or an opinion of choice.

a. Power III
b. Decision making
c. 6-3-5 Brainwriting
d. 180SearchAssistant

20. In economics, _________ are business expenses that are not dependent on the activities of the business They tend to be time-related, such as salaries or rents being paid per month. This is in contrast to variable costs, which are volume-related (and are paid per quantity.)

In management accounting, _________ are defined as expenses that do not change in proportion to the activity of a business, within the relevant period or scale of production.

a. Variable cost
b. Transaction cost
c. Marginal cost
d. Fixed Costs

21. _________ is a rivalry between individuals, groups, nations for territory, a niche, or allocation of resources. It arises whenever two or more parties strive for a goal which cannot be shared. _________ occurs naturally between living organisms which co-exist in the same environment.

a. Competition
b. Price competition
c. Non-price competition
d. Price fixing

22. _________ is a term used in business to indicate a state of intense competitive rivalry accompanied by a multi-lateral series of price reduction. One competitor will lower its price, then others will lower their prices to match. If one of them reduces their price again, a new round of reductions starts.

a. Pricing objectives
b. Competitor indexing
c. Resale price maintenance
d. Price war

23. A _________ is a collection of symbols, experiences and associations connected with a product, a service, a person or any other artifact or entity.

_________s have become increasingly important components of culture and the economy, now being described as 'cultural accessories and personal philosophies'.

Some people distinguish the psychological aspect of a _________ from the experiential aspect.

a. Store brand
b. Brand
c. Brand equity
d. Brandable software

24. _________ is a broad label that refers to any individuals or households that use goods and services generated within the economy. The concept of a _________ is used in different contexts, so that the usage and significance of the term may vary.

A _________ is a person who uses any product or service.

a. 180SearchAssistant
b. Power III
c. 6-3-5 Brainwriting
d. Consumer

25. _________ is a form of government regulation which protects the interests of consumers. For example, a government may require businesses to disclose detailed information about products--particularly in areas where safety or public health is an issue, such as food. _________ is linked to the idea of consumer rights (that consumers have various rights as consumers), and to the formation of consumer organizations which help consumers make better choices in the marketplace.

a. Consumer protection
b. Trademark dilution
c. Sound trademark
d. Federal Bureau of Investigation

26. _________ is one of the four growth strategies of the Product-Market Growth Matrix defined by Ansoff. _________ occurs when a company enters/penetrates a market with current products. The best way to achieve this is by gaining competitors' customers (part of their market share.)

a. Pasar pagi
b. Horizontal market
c. Marketization
d. Market penetration

27. _________ is the economic policy of restraining trade between nations, through methods such as tariffs on imported goods, restrictive quotas, and a variety of other restrictive government regulations designed to discourage imports, and prevent foreign take-over of local markets and companies. This policy is closely aligned with anti-globalization, and contrasts with free trade, where government barriers to trade are kept to a minimum. The term is mostly used in the context of economics, where _________ refers to policies or doctrines which 'protect' businesses and workers within a country by restricting or regulating trade with foreign nations.

a. Market economy
b. Gift economy
c. Black market
d. Protectionism

28. A grey market or _________ is the trade of a commodity through distribution channels which, while legal, are unofficial, unauthorized, or unintended by the original manufacturer. In contrast, a black market is the trade of goods and services that are illegal in themselves and/or distributed through illegal channels, such as the selling of stolen goods or illegal items such as heroin or unregistered handguns.

The two main types of grey market are imported manufactured goods that would be normally unavailable or more expensive in a certain country and unissued securities that are not yet traded in official markets.

a. Zone pricing
b. Green market
c. Customs union
d. Gray market

29. _________ is a common market form. Many markets can be considered monopolistically competitive, often including the markets for restaurants, cereal, clothing, shoes and service industries in large cities. Short-run equilibrium of the firm under _________

Monopolistically competitive markets have the following characteristics:

- There are many producers and many consumers in a given market, and no business has total control over the market price.
- Consumers perceive that there are non-price differences among the competitors' products.
- There are few barriers to entry and exit.
- Producers have a degree of control over price.

Long-run equilibrium of the firm under _________

The characteristics of a monopolistically competitive market are almost the same as in perfect competition, with the exception of heterogeneous products, and that _________ involves a great deal of non-price competition (based on subtle product differentiation.) A firm making profits in the short run will break even in the long run because demand will decrease and average total cost will increase.

a. Monopolistic competition
b. Gross domestic product
c. Recession
d. Macroeconomics

30. _________ is the ability of an individual or group to seclude themselves or information about themselves and thereby reveal themselves selectively. The boundaries and content of what is considered private differ among cultures and individuals, but share basic common themes. _________ is sometimes related to anonymity, the wish to remain unnoticed or unidentified in the public realm.

a. Privacy
b. Power III
c. 6-3-5 Brainwriting
d. 180SearchAssistant

31. _________s is the social science that studies the production, distribution, and consumption of goods and services. The term _________s comes from the Ancient Greek οá¼°κονομÎ¯α from οá¼¶κος (oikos, 'house') + vÏŒμος (nomos, 'custom' or 'law'), hence 'rules of the house(hold)'. Current _________ models developed out of the broader field of political economy in the late 19th century, owing to a desire to use an empirical approach more akin to the physical sciences.

a. Economic
b. Industrial organization
c. ADTECH
d. ACNielsen

32. _________ is a form of communication that typically attempts to persuade potential customers to purchase or to consume more of a particular brand of product or service. 'While now central to the contemporary global economy and the reproduction of global production networks, it is only quite recently that _________ has been more than a marginal influence on patterns of sales and production. The formation of modern _________ was intimately bound up with the emergence of new forms of monopoly capitalism around the end of the 19th and beginning of the 20th century as one element in corporate strategies to create, organize and where possible control markets, especially for mass produced consumer goods.

a. AMAX
b. ADTECH
c. ACNielsen
d. Advertising

1. _________ is one of the four Ps of the marketing mix. The other three aspects are product, promotion, and place. It is also a key variable in microeconomic price allocation theory.

a. Pricing
b. Price
c. Competitor indexing
d. Relationship based pricing

2. _________ is the practice of keeping the price of a product or service artificially high in order to encourage favorable perceptions among buyers, based solely on the price. The practice is intended to exploit the (not necessarily justifiable) tendency for buyers to assume that expensive items enjoy an exceptional reputation or represent exceptional quality and distinction.

The use of _________ as either a marketing strategy or a competitive practice depends on certain factors that influence its profitability and sustainability.

a. Target costing
b. Price maintenance
c. Price war
d. Premium pricing

3. _________, or Value optimized pricing is a business strategy. It sets selling prices on the perceived value to the customer, rather than on the actual cost of the product, the market price, competitors prices, or the historical price.

The goal of _________ is to align price with value delivered.

a. Service-profit chain
b. Value-based pricing
c. Jobbing house
d. Money back guarantee

4. In economics, business, retail, and accounting, a _________ is the value of money that has been used up to produce something, and hence is not available for use anymore. In economics, a _________ is an alternative that is given up as a result of a decision. In business, the _________ may be one of acquisition, in which case the amount of money expended to acquire it is counted as _________.

a. Variable cost
b. Cost
c. Transaction cost
d. Fixed costs

5. _________ is the state or fact of exclusive rights and control over property, which may be an object, land/real estate, or some other kind of property (like government-granted monopolies collectively referred to as intellectual property.) It is embodied in an _________ right also referred to as title.

_________ is the key building block in the development of the capitalist socio-economic system.

a. ADTECH
b. ACNielsen
c. AMAX
d. Ownership

6. A personal and cultural _________ is a relative ethic _________, an assumption upon which implementation can be extrapolated. A _________ system is a set of consistent _________s and measures that is soo not true. A principle _________ is a foundation upon which other _________s and measures of integrity are based.

a. Supreme Court of the United States
b. Perceptual maps
c. Value
d. Package-on-Package

7. In economics, an externality or spillover of an economic transaction is an impact on a party that is not directly involved in the transaction. In such a case, prices do not reflect the full costs or benefits in production or consumption of a product or service. A positive impact is called an _________ benefit, while a negative impact is called an _________ cost.

a. AMAX
b. ACNielsen
c. ADTECH
d. External

8. _________ can be regarded as an outcome of mental processes (cognitive process) leading to the selection of a course of action among several alternatives. Every _________ process produces a final choice. The output can be an action or an opinion of choice.

a. 180SearchAssistant
b. Power III
c. 6-3-5 Brainwriting
d. Decision making

9. _________ in economics and business is the result of an exchange and from that trade we assign a numerical monetary value to a good, service or asset. If I trade 4 apples for an orange, the _________ of an orange is 4 - apples. Inversely, the _________ of an apple is 1/4 oranges.

a. Pricing
b. Price
c. Contribution margin-based pricing
d. Discounts and allowances

10. _________ is a pricing strategy in which a marketer sets a relatively high price for a product or service at first, then lowers the price over time. It is a temporal version of price discrimination/yield management. It allows the firm to recover its sunk costs quickly before competition steps in and lowers the market price.

a. Price markdown
b. Discounts and allowances
c. Relationship based pricing
d. Price skimming

11. In business and engineering, new _________ is the term used to describe the complete process of bringing a new product or service to market. There are two parallel paths involved in the Nproduct development process: one involves the idea generation, product design, and detail engineering; the other involves market research and marketing analysis. Companies typically see new _________ as the first stage in generating and commercializing new products within the overall strategic process of product life cycle management used to maintain or grow their market share.

a. Specification tree
b. New product screening
c. Product development
d. New product development

12. _________ is one of the four growth strategies of the Product-Market Growth Matrix defined by Ansoff. _________ occurs when a company enters/penetrates a market with current products. The best way to achieve this is by gaining competitors' customers (part of their market share.)

a. Market penetration
b. Pasar pagi
c. Marketization
d. Horizontal market

13. A _________ is a plan of action designed to achieve a particular goal.

_________ is different from tactics. In military terms, tactics is concerned with the conduct of an engagement while _________ is concerned with how different engagements are linked.

a. Strategy
b. Power III
c. 6-3-5 Brainwriting
d. 180SearchAssistant

14. _________ is a term commonly used to describe commerce transactions between businesses like the one between a manufacturer and a wholesaler or a wholesaler and a retailer i.e both the buyer and the seller are business entity.This is unlike business-to-consumers (B2C) which involve a business entity and end consumer, or business-to-government (B2G) which involve a business entity and government.

The volume of B2B transactions is much higher than the volume of B2C transactions. The primary reason for this is that in a typical supply chain there will be many B2B transactions involving subcomponent or raw materials, and only one B2C transaction, specifically sale of the finished product to the end customer.

a. Customer relationship management
b. Social marketing
c. Disruptive technology
d. Business-to-business

15. _________ is a form of communication that typically attempts to persuade potential customers to purchase or to consume more of a particular brand of product or service. 'While now central to the contemporary global economy and the reproduction of global production networks, it is only quite recently that _________ has been more than a marginal influence on patterns of sales and production. The formation of modern _________ was intimately bound up with the emergence of new forms of monopoly capitalism around the end of the 19th and beginning of the 20th century as one element in corporate strategies to create, organize and where possible control markets, especially for mass produced consumer goods.

a. ADTECH
b. ACNielsen
c. AMAX
d. Advertising

16. _________ is a broad label that refers to any individuals or households that use goods and services generated within the economy. The concept of a _________ is used in different contexts, so that the usage and significance of the term may vary.

A _________ is a person who uses any product or service.

a. 180SearchAssistant
b. Consumer
c. Power III
d. 6-3-5 Brainwriting

17. In marketing a _________ is a ticket or document that can be exchanged for a financial discount or rebate when purchasing a product. Customarily, _________s are issued by manufacturers of consumer packaged goods or by retailers, to be used in retail stores as a part of sales promotions. They are often widely distributed through mail, magazines, newspapers, the Internet, and mobile devices such as cell phones.

a. Merchandise
b. Marketing communication
c. Merchandising
d. Coupon

18. _________ is a lightweight markup language, originally created by John Gruber and Aaron Swartz to help maximum readability and 'publishability' of both its input and output forms. The language takes many cues from existing conventions for marking up plain text in email. _________ converts its marked-up text input to valid, well-formed XHTML and replaces left-pointing angle brackets ('<') and ampersands with their corresponding character entity references.

a. 180SearchAssistant
b. 6-3-5 Brainwriting
c. Power III
d. Markdown

19. A _________ is an amount paid by way of reduction, return, or refund on what has already been paid or contributed. It is a type of sales promotion marketers use primarily as incentives or supplements to product sales. The mail-in _________ is the most common.

a. Strand
b. Lifestyle city
c. Personalization
d. Rebate

20. False advertising or _________ is the use of false or misleading statements in advertising. As advertising has the potential to persuade people into commercial transactions that they might otherwise avoid, many governments around the world use regulations to control false, deceptive or misleading advertising. Truth in labeling refers to essentially the same concept, that customers have the right to know what they are buying, and that all necessary information should be on the label.

a. Misleading advertising
b. Fine print
c. Deceptive advertising
d. Power III

21. _________ is a branch of philosophy which seeks to address questions about morality, such as how a moral outcome can be achieved in a specific situation (applied _________), how moral values should be determined (normative _________), what moral values people actually abide by (descriptive _________), what the fundamental semantic, ontological, and epistemic nature of _________ or morality is (meta-_________), and how moral capacity or moral agency develops and what its nature is (moral psychology.)

Socrates was one of the first Greek philosophers to encourage both scholars and the common citizen to turn their attention from the outside world to the condition of man. In this view, Knowledge having a bearing on human life was placed highest, all other knowledge being secondary.

a. Ethics
b. ADTECH
c. AMAX
d. ACNielsen

22. _________ is one of the four aspects of promotional mix. (The other three parts of the promotional mix are advertising, personal selling, and publicity/public relations.) Media and non-media marketing communication are employed for a pre-determined, limited time to increase consumer demand, stimulate market demand or improve product availability.

a. Sales promotion
b. Merchandise
c. New Media Strategies
d. Marketing communication

23. _________ generally refers to a list of all planned expenses and revenues. It is a plan for saving and spending. A _________ is an important concept in microeconomics, which uses a _________ line to illustrate the trade-offs between two or more goods.

a. 180SearchAssistant
b. 6-3-5 Brainwriting
c. Power III
d. Budget

24. _________ , according to The American Marketing Association, is 'a planning process designed to assure that all brand contacts received by a customer or prospect for a product, service, or organization are relevant to that person and consistent over time.' (Marketing Power Dictionary)

_________ is a term used to describe a holistic approach to marketing. It aims to ensure consistency of message and the complementary use of media. The concept includes online and offline marketing channels.

a. ACNielsen
b. ADTECH
c. AMAX
d. Integrated marketing communications

25. _________ is defined by the American _________ Association as the activity, set of institutions, and processes for creating, communicating, delivering, and exchanging offerings that have value for customers, clients, partners, and society at large. The term developed from the original meaning which referred literally to going to market, as in shopping, or going to a market to sell goods or services.

_________ practice tends to be seen as a creative industry, which includes advertising, distribution and selling.

a. Marketing myopia
b. Customer acquisition management
c. Product naming
d. Marketing

26. _________ refers to messages and related media used to communicate with a market. Those who practice advertising, branding, direct marketing, graphic design, marketing, packaging, promotion, publicity, sponsorship, public relations, sales, sales promotion and online marketing are termed marketing communicators, _________ managers, or more briefly as marcom managers.

a. Marketing communication
b. Sales promotion
c. Merchandising
d. Merchandise

27. _________ is the pricing technique of setting a relatively low initial entry price, often lower than the eventual market price, to attract new customers. The strategy works on the expectation that customers will switch to the new brand because of the lower price. _________ is most commonly associated with a marketing objective of increasing market share or sales volume, rather than to make profit in the short term.

a. Fee
b. Competitor indexing
c. Price war
d. Penetration pricing

28. _________ involves disseminating information about a product, product line, brand, or company. It is one of the four key aspects of the marketing mix. (The other three elements are product marketing, pricing, and distribution). P>_________ is generally sub-divided into two parts:

- Above the line _________: Promotion in the media (e.g. TV, radio, newspapers, Internet and Mobile Phones) in which the advertiser pays an advertising agency to place the ad
- Below the line _________: All other _________. Much of this is intended to be subtle enough for the consumer to be unaware that _________ is taking place. E.g. sponsorship, product placement, endorsements, sales _________, merchandising, direct mail, personal selling, public relations, trade shows

a. Cashmere Agency
b. Bottling lines
c. Davie Brown Index
d. Promotion

29. Competitiveness is a comparative concept of the ability and performance of a firm, sub-sector or country to sell and supply goods and/or services in a given market. Although widely used in economics and business management, the usefulness of the concept, particularly in the context of national competitiveness, is vigorously disputed by economists, such as Paul Krugman .

The term may also be applied to markets, where it is used to refer to the extent to which the market structure may be regarded as perfectly _________.

a. Geographical pricing
b. Customs union
c. Free trade zone
d. Competitive

30. A _________ or leader is a product sold at a low price (at cost or below cost) to stimulate other, profitable sales. It is a kind of sales promotion, in other words marketing concentrating on a pricing strategy. The price can even be so low that the product is sold at a loss.

a. Resale price maintenance
b. Penetration pricing
c. Price shading
d. Loss leader

31. _________ is the practice of selling a product or service at a very low price, intending to drive competitors out of the market, or create barriers to entry for potential new competitors. If competitors or potential competitors cannot sustain equal or lower prices without losing money, they go out of business or choose not to enter the business. The predatory merchant then has fewer competitors or is even a de facto monopoly, and can then raise prices above what the market would otherwise bear.

a. Predatory pricing
b. List price
c. Power III
d. 180SearchAssistant

32. _________ exists when sales of identical goods or services are transacted at different prices from the same provider. In a theoretical market with perfect information, no transaction costs or prohibition on secondary exchange (or re-selling) to prevent arbitrage, _________ can only be a feature of monopoly and oligopoly markets, where market power can be exercised. Otherwise, the moment the seller tries to sell the same good at different prices, the buyer at the lower price can arbitrage by selling to the consumer buying at the higher price but with a tiny discount.

a. Resale price maintenance
b. Price discrimination
c. Penetration pricing
d. Price

33. The _________ of 1936 (or Anti-Price Discrimination Act, 15 U.S.C. Â§ 13) is a United States federal law that prohibits what were considered, at the time of passage, to be anticompetitive practices by producers, specifically price discrimination. It grew out of practices in which chain stores were allowed to purchase goods at lower prices than other retailers.

a. Robinson-Patman Act
b. Fair Debt Collection Practices Act
c. Registered trademark symbol
d. Trademark infringement

34. The _________ requires the Federal government to investigate and pursue trusts, companies and organizations suspected of violating the Act. It was the first United States Federal statute to limit cartels and monopolies, and today still forms the basis for most antitrust litigation by the federal government.

a. Power III
b. 6-3-5 Brainwriting
c. 180SearchAssistant
d. Sherman Antitrust Act

35. _________ is a form of government regulation which protects the interests of consumers. For example, a government may require businesses to disclose detailed information about products--particularly in areas where safety or public health is an issue, such as food. _________ is linked to the idea of consumer rights (that consumers have various rights as consumers), and to the formation of consumer organizations which help consumers make better choices in the marketplace.

a. Sound trademark
b. Federal Bureau of Investigation
c. Trademark dilution
d. Consumer protection

36. An _________ is a situation that will often involve an apparent conflict between moral imperatives, in which to obey one would result in transgressing another. This is also called an ethical paradox since in moral philosophy, paradox plays a central role in ethics debates. For instance, an ethical admonition to 'love thy neighbour as thy self' is not always just in contrast with, but sometimes in contradiction to an armed neighbour actively trying to kill you: if he or she succeeds, you will not be able to love him or her.

a. ACNielsen
b. AMAX
c. ADTECH
d. Ethical dilemma

37. _________ is an agreement between business competitors to sell the same product or service at the same price. In general, it is an agreement intended to ultimately push the price of a product as high as possible, leading to profits for all the sellers. _________ can also involve any agreement to fix, peg, discount or stabilize prices.

a. Price competition
b. Direct competition
c. Non-price competition
d. Price fixing

1. A _________ or logistics network is the system of organizations, people, technology, activities, information and resources involved in moving a product or service from supplier to customer. _________ activities transform natural resources, raw materials and components into a finished product that is delivered to the end customer. In sophisticated _________ systems, used products may re-enter the _________ at any point where residual value is recyclable.

a. Supply chain
b. Demand chain management
c. Supply chain network
d. Purchasing

2. In operant conditioning, _________ occurs when an event following a response causes an increase in the probability of that response occurring in the future. Response strength can be assessed by measures such as the frequency with which the response is made (for example, a pigeon may peck a key more times in the session), or the speed with which it is made (for example, a rat may run a maze faster.) The environment change contingent upon the response is called a reinforcer.

a. Generic brands
b. Completely randomized designs
c. Relationship Management Application
d. Reinforcement

3. A personal and cultural _________ is a relative ethic _________, an assumption upon which implementation can be extrapolated. A _________ system is a set of consistent _________s and measures that is soo not true. A principle _________ is a foundation upon which other _________s and measures of integrity are based.

a. Supreme Court of the United States
b. Perceptual maps
c. Value
d. Package-on-Package

4. _________ is defined by the American _________ Association as the activity, set of institutions, and processes for creating, communicating, delivering, and exchanging offerings that have value for customers, clients, partners, and society at large. The term developed from the original meaning which referred literally to going to market, as in shopping, or going to a market to sell goods or services.

_________ practice tends to be seen as a creative industry, which includes advertising, distribution and selling.

a. Product naming
b. Marketing myopia
c. Customer acquisition management
d. Marketing

5. The _________ of 1938 is a United States federal law that amended the Federal Trade Commission Act to add the clause 'unfair or deceptive acts or practices in commerce are hereby declared unlawful' to the Section 5 prohibition of unfair methods of competition, in order to protect consumers as well as competition.

1938 amendment to the federal trade commission act that authorized the FTC to restrict unfair or deceptive acts; also called the advertising act. Until this amendment was passed, the FTC could only restrict practices that were unfair to competitors.

a. Patent
b. Sarbanes-Oxley Act of 2002
c. Nutrition Labeling and Education Act
d. Wheeler-Lea Act

6. _________ is the management of the flow of goods, information and other resources, including energy and people, between the point of origin and the point of consumption in order to meet the requirements of consumers (frequently, and originally, military organizations.) _________ involves the integration of information, transportation, inventory, warehousing, material-handling, and packaging. _________ is a channel of the supply chain which adds the value of time and place utility.

a. Power III
b. Logistics
c. 6-3-5 Brainwriting
d. 180SearchAssistant

7. the term _________ is that part of Supply Chain Management that plans, implements, and controls the efficient, effective, forward, and reverse flow and storage of goods, services, and related information between the point of origin and the point of consumption in order to meet customers' requirements.

Software is used for logistics automation which helps the supply chain industry in automating the work flow as well as management of the system. There are very few generalized software available in the new market in the said topology.

a. Digital strategy
b. Corporate transparency
c. Crisis management
d. Logistics management

8. _________ is one of the four elements of marketing mix. An organization or set of organizations (go-betweens) involved in the process of making a product or service available for use or consumption by a consumer or business user.

The other three parts of the marketing mix are product, pricing, and promotion.

a. Comparison-Shopping agent
b. Distribution
c. Better Living Through Chemistry
d. Japan Advertising Photographers' Association

9. A _________ is a collection of symbols, experiences and associations connected with a product, a service, a person or any other artifact or entity.

_________s have become increasingly important components of culture and the economy, now being described as 'cultural accessories and personal philosophies'.

Some people distinguish the psychological aspect of a _________ from the experiential aspect.

a. Brand equity
b. Brandable software
c. Store brand
d. Brand

10. A _________ for a set of products is a warehouse or other specialized building, often with refrigeration or air conditioning, which is stocked with products (goods) to be re-distributed to retailers, wholesalers or directly to consumers. A _________ is a principle part, the 'order processing' element, of the entire 'order fulfillment' process. _________s are usually thought of as being 'demand driven'.

a. Distribution center
b. 180SearchAssistant
c. Power III
d. 6-3-5 Brainwriting

11. _________ refers to the structured transmission of data between organizations by electronic means. It is used to transfer electronic documents from one computer system to another (ie) from one trading partner to another trading partner. It is more than mere E-mail; for instance, organizations might replace bills of lading and even checks with appropriate _________ messages.

a. AMAX
b. Electronic data interchange
c. ACNielsen
d. ADTECH

12. _________ refer to a collection of facts usually collected as the result of experience, observation or experiment or a set of premises. This may consist of numbers, words particularly as measurements or observations of a set of variables. _________ are often viewed as a lowest level of abstraction from which information and knowledge are derived.

a. Mean
b. Pearson product-moment correlation coefficient
c. Sample size
d. Data

13. Merchandising refers to the methods, practices and operations conducted to promote and sustain certain categories of commercial activity. The term is understood to have different specific meanings depending on the context. _________ is a sale goods at a store

In marketing, one of the definitions of merchandising is the practice in which the brand or image from one product or service is used to sell another.

a. Merchandise
b. New Media Strategies
c. Sales promotion
d. Merchandising

14. _________ is a practice in logistics of unloading materials from an incoming semi-trailer truck or rail car and loading these materials in outbound trailers or rail cars, with little or no storage in between. This may be done to change type of conveyance, or to sort material intended for different destinations, or to combine material from different origins.

In purest form this is done directly, with minimal or no warehousing.

a. Customer base
b. Cross-docking
c. Product life cycle management
d. Product support

15. Radio-frequency identification (_________) is the use of an object (typically referred to as an _________ tag) applied to or incorporated into a product, animal, or person for the purpose of identification and tracking using radio waves. Some tags can be read from several meters away and beyond the line of sight of the reader.

Most _________ tags contain at least two parts.

a. 6-3-5 Brainwriting
b. 180SearchAssistant
c. Power III
d. RFID

16. _________ is a list for goods and materials held available in stock by a business. It is also used for a list of the contents of a household and for a list for testamentary purposes of the possessions of someone who has died. In accounting _________ is considered an asset.

a. ADTECH
b. ACNielsen
c. Ending Inventory
d. Inventory

17. _________ is an inventory strategy implemented to improve the return on investment of a business by reducing in-process inventory and its associated carrying costs. In order to achieve JIT the process must have signals of what is going on elsewhere within the process. This means that the process is often driven by a series of signals, which can be Kanban , that tell production processes when to make the next part.

a. Just-in-time
b. Clutter
c. Personalization
d. Promotion

18. In economics, _________ is the desire to own something and the ability to pay for it. The term _________ signifies the ability or the willingness to buy a particular commodity at a given point of time .

.

a. Discretionary spending
b. Market dominance
c. Market system
d. Demand

19. In economics, the _________ can be defined as the graph depicting the relationship between the price of a certain commodity, and the amount of it that consumers are willing and able to purchase at that given price. It is a graphic representation of a demand schedule The _________ for all consumers together follows from the _________ of every individual consumer: the individual demands at each price are added together.

_________s are used to estimate behaviors in competitive markets, and are often combined with supply curves to estimate the equilibrium price (the price at which sellers together are willing to sell the same amount as buyers together are willing to buy, also known as market clearing price) and the equilibrium quantity (the amount of that good or service that will be produced and bought without surplus/excess supply or shortage/excess demand) of that market.

a. 180SearchAssistant
b. Demand curve
c. Power III
d. 6-3-5 Brainwriting

20. _________ is one of the four Ps of the marketing mix. The other three aspects are product, promotion, and place. It is also a key variable in microeconomic price allocation theory.

a. Relationship based pricing
b. Competitor indexing
c. Price
d. Pricing

21. _________ is the study of the Earth and its lands, features, inhabitants, and phenomena. A literal translation would be 'to describe or write about the Earth'. The first person to use the word '_________' was Eratosthenes .

a. Geography
b. 6-3-5 Brainwriting
c. Power III
d. 180SearchAssistant

22. _________ occurs when manufacturers (brands) disintermediate their channel partners, such as distributors, retailers, dealers, and sales representatives, by selling their products direct to consumers through general marketing methods and/or over the internet through eCommerce.

Some manufacturers want their brands to capture the power of the internet but do not want to create conflict with their other distribution channels, as these partners are necessary and viable for any manufacturer to maintain and gain success. The Census Bureau of the U.S. Department of Commerce reported that online sales in 2005 grew 24.6 percent over 2004 to reach 86.3 billion dollars.

a. Store brand
b. Retail design
c. Trade Symbols
d. Channel conflict

23. The most important feature of a contract is that one party makes an _________ for an arrangement that another accepts. This can be called a 'concurrence of wills' or 'ad idem' (meeting of the minds) of two or more parties. The concept is somewhat contested.

a. Offer
b. AMAX
c. ACNielsen
d. ADTECH

24. _________ refers to the methods of practicing and using another person's philosophy of business. The franchisor grants the independent operator the right to distribute its products, techniques, and trademarks for a percentage of gross monthly sales and a royalty fee. Various tangibles and intangibles such as national or international advertising, training, and other support services are commonly made available by the franchisor.

a. 180SearchAssistant
b. Power III
c. Franchise fee
d. Franchising

25. The _________ is generally accepted as the use and specification of the four p's describing the strategic position of a product in the marketplace. One version of the origins of the _________ starts in 1948 when James Culliton said that a marketing decision should be a result of something similar to a recipe. This version continued in 1953 when Neil Borden, in his American Marketing Association presidential address, took the recipe idea one step further and coined the term 'Marketing-Mix'.

a. Power III
b. 180SearchAssistant
c. 6-3-5 Brainwriting
d. Marketing mix

26. _________ is a form of communication that typically attempts to persuade potential customers to purchase or to consume more of a particular brand of product or service. 'While now central to the contemporary global economy and the reproduction of global production networks, it is only quite recently that _________ has been more than a marginal influence on patterns of sales and production. The formation of modern _________ was intimately bound up with the emergence of new forms of monopoly capitalism around the end of the 19th and beginning of the 20th century as one element in corporate strategies to create, organize and where possible control markets, especially for mass produced consumer goods.

a. AMAX
b. Advertising
c. ACNielsen
d. ADTECH

1. The _________ of 1938 is a United States federal law that amended the Federal Trade Commission Act to add the clause 'unfair or deceptive acts or practices in commerce are hereby declared unlawful' to the Section 5 prohibition of unfair methods of competition, in order to protect consumers as well as competition.

1938 amendment to the federal trade commission act that authorized the FTC to restrict unfair or deceptive acts; also called the advertising act. Until this amendment was passed, the FTC could only restrict practices that were unfair to competitors.

a. Sarbanes-Oxley Act of 2002
b. Wheeler-Lea Act
c. Nutrition Labeling and Education Act
d. Patent

2. A personal and cultural _________ is a relative ethic _________, an assumption upon which implementation can be extrapolated. A _________ system is a set of consistent _________s and measures that is soo not true. A principle _________ is a foundation upon which other _________s and measures of integrity are based.

a. Perceptual maps
b. Package-on-Package
c. Supreme Court of the United States
d. Value

3. A _________ is a collection of symbols, experiences and associations connected with a product, a service, a person or any other artifact or entity.

_________s have become increasingly important components of culture and the economy, now being described as 'cultural accessories and personal philosophies'.

Some people distinguish the psychological aspect of a _________ from the experiential aspect.

a. Store brand
b. Brandable software
c. Brand equity
d. Brand

4. _________ is defined by the American _________ Association as the activity, set of institutions, and processes for creating, communicating, delivering, and exchanging offerings that have value for customers, clients, partners, and society at large. The term developed from the original meaning which referred literally to going to market, as in shopping, or going to a market to sell goods or services.

_________ practice tends to be seen as a creative industry, which includes advertising, distribution and selling.

a. Product naming
b. Marketing
c. Customer acquisition management
d. Marketing myopia

5. The _________ is generally accepted as the use and specification of the four p's describing the strategic position of a product in the marketplace. One version of the origins of the _________ starts in 1948 when James Culliton said that a marketing decision should be a result of something similar to a recipe. This version continued in 1953 when Neil Borden, in his American Marketing Association presidential address, took the recipe idea one step further and coined the term 'Marketing-Mix'.

a. Marketing mix
b. 6-3-5 Brainwriting
c. 180SearchAssistant
d. Power III

6. _________ in economics and business is the result of an exchange and from that trade we assign a numerical monetary value to a good, service or asset. If I trade 4 apples for an orange, the _________ of an orange is 4 - apples. Inversely, the _________ of an apple is 1/4 oranges.

a. Discounts and allowances
b. Pricing
c. Contribution margin-based pricing
d. Price

7. In business and engineering, new _________ is the term used to describe the complete process of bringing a new product or service to market. There are two parallel paths involved in the Nproduct development process: one involves the idea generation, product design, and detail engineering; the other involves market research and marketing analysis. Companies typically see new _________ as the first stage in generating and commercializing new products within the overall strategic process of product life cycle management used to maintain or grow their market share.

a. Product development
b. Specification tree
c. New product development
d. New product screening

8. _________s (house brands in the United States, own brands in the UK, and home brands in Australia) are brands which are specific to a retail store or store chain. The retailer can manufacture goods under its own label, re-brand private label goods, or outsource manufacture of _________ items to multiple third parties - often the same manufacturers that produce brand label goods. _________ goods are generally cheaper than national brand goods because the retailer can optimize the production to suit consumer demand and reduce advertising costs.

a. Brand strength analysis
b. Store brand
c. Brand loyalty
d. Brand ambassador

9. _________ is a rivalry between individuals, groups, nations for territory, a niche, or allocation of resources. It arises whenever two or more parties strive for a goal which cannot be shared. _________ occurs naturally between living organisms which co-exist in the same environment.

a. Competition
b. Price competition
c. Price fixing
d. Non-price competition

10. _________ is one of the four Ps of the marketing mix. The other three aspects are product, promotion, and place. It is also a key variable in microeconomic price allocation theory.

a. Pricing
b. Relationship based pricing
c. Price
d. Competitor indexing

11. _________ deals with the first of the '4P''s of marketing, which are Product, Pricing, Place, and Promotion. _________, as opposed to product management, deals with more outbound marketing tasks. For example, product management deals with the nuts and bolts of product development within a firm, whereas _________ deals with marketing the product to prospects, customers, and others.

a. Reverse hierarchy
b. Corporate transparency
c. Crisis management
d. Product Marketing

12. _________ consists of the sale of goods or merchandise from a fixed location, such as a department store or kiosk in small or individual lots for direct consumption by the purchaser. _________ may include subordinated services, such as delivery. Purchasers may be individuals or businesses.

a. Warehouse store
b. Charity shop
c. Thrifting
d. Retailing

13. _________ is subcontracting a process, such as product design or manufacturing, to a third-party company. The decision to outsource is often made in the interest of lowering cost or making better use of time and energy costs, redirecting or conserving energy directed at the competencies of a particular business, or to make more efficient use of land, labor, capital, (information) technology and resources. _________ became part of the business lexicon during the 1980s.

a. Outsourcing
b. In-house
c. ACNielsen
d. Intangible assets

14. _________ is one of the four growth strategies of the Product-Market Growth Matrix defined by Ansoff. _________ occurs when a company enters/penetrates a market with current products. The best way to achieve this is by gaining competitors' customers (part of their market share.)

a. Horizontal market
b. Pasar pagi
c. Market penetration
d. Marketization

15. _________ , according to The American Marketing Association, is 'a planning process designed to assure that all brand contacts received by a customer or prospect for a product, service, or organization are relevant to that person and consistent over time.' (Marketing Power Dictionary)

_________ is a term used to describe a holistic approach to marketing. It aims to ensure consistency of message and the complementary use of media. The concept includes online and offline marketing channels.

a. AMAX
b. ACNielsen
c. ADTECH
d. Integrated marketing communications

16. _________ involves disseminating information about a product, product line, brand, or company. It is one of the four key aspects of the marketing mix. (The other three elements are product marketing, pricing, and distribution). P>_________ is generally sub-divided into two parts:

- Above the line _________: Promotion in the media (e.g. TV, radio, newspapers, Internet and Mobile Phones) in which the advertiser pays an advertising agency to place the ad
- Below the line _________: All other _________. Much of this is intended to be subtle enough for the consumer to be unaware that _________ is taking place. E.g. sponsorship, product placement, endorsements, sales _________, merchandising, direct mail, personal selling, public relations, trade shows

a. Bottling lines
b. Cashmere Agency
c. Promotion
d. Davie Brown Index

17. _________ is a broad label that refers to any individuals or households that use goods and services generated within the economy. The concept of a _________ is used in different contexts, so that the usage and significance of the term may vary.

A _________ is a person who uses any product or service.

a. Power III
b. 180SearchAssistant
c. 6-3-5 Brainwriting
d. Consumer

18. _________ is the study of when, why, how, where and what people do or do not buy products. It blends elements from psychology, sociology,social psychology, anthropology and economics. It attempts to understand the buyer decision making process, both individually and in groups. It studies characteristics of individual consumers such as demographics and behavioural variables in an attempt to understand people's wants. It also tries to assess influences on the consumer from groups such as family, friends, reference groups, and society in general.

a. Communal marketing
b. Multidimensional scaling
c. Consumer confidence
d. Consumer behavior

19. _________ refers to messages and related media used to communicate with a market. Those who practice advertising, branding, direct marketing, graphic design, marketing, packaging, promotion, publicity, sponsorship, public relations, sales, sales promotion and online marketing are termed marketing communicators, _________ managers, or more briefly as marcom managers.

a. Merchandising
b. Merchandise
c. Marketing communication
d. Sales promotion

20. A _________ or logistics network is the system of organizations, people, technology, activities, information and resources involved in moving a product or service from supplier to customer. _________ activities transform natural resources, raw materials and components into a finished product that is delivered to the end customer. In sophisticated _________ systems, used products may re-enter the _________ at any point where residual value is recyclable.

a. Supply chain network
b. Demand chain management
c. Purchasing
d. Supply chain

21. A _________ is a company that sells directly to the public via more than one distribution channel. Most _________s sell through mail order catalogs and 'brick ' mortar' retail stores. Some _________s, sell online as well.

a. Khodebshchik
b. Gruen transfer
c. Discount store
d. Multichannel retailer

22. _________ is anything that is intended to save time, energy or frustration. A _________ store at a petrol station, for example, sells items that have nothing to do with gasoline/petrol, but it saves the consumer from having to go to a grocery store. '_________' is a very relative term and its meaning tends to change over time.

a. Demographic profile
b. MaxDiff
c. Marketing buzz
d. Convenience

23. A _________ is a small store or shop that sells candy, ice-cream, soft drinks, lottery tickets, newspapers and magazines, along with a small selection of food and grocery supplies. Stores that are part of gas stations may also sell motor oil, windshield washer fluid, radiator fluid, and maps. Often toiletries and other hygiene products are stocked, and some of these stores also offer money orders and wire transfer services or liquor products.

a. 180SearchAssistant
b. Power III
c. 6-3-5 Brainwriting
d. Convenience store

24. Merchandising refers to the methods, practices and operations conducted to promote and sustain certain categories of commercial activity. The term is understood to have different specific meanings depending on the context. _________ is a sale goods at a store

In marketing, one of the definitions of merchandising is the practice in which the brand or image from one product or service is used to sell another.

a. Merchandising
b. Sales promotion
c. New Media Strategies
d. Merchandise

25. A _________ is a type of department store, which sell products at prices lower than those asked by traditional retail outlets. Most discount department stores offer wide assortments of goods; others specialize in such merchandise as jewelry, electronic equipment, or electrical appliances. _________s are not dollar stores, which sell goods at a dollar or less.

a. Gruen transfer
b. Sales per unit area
c. Strip mall
d. Discount store

26. _________ are small stores which specialize in a specific range of merchandise and related items. Most stores have an extensive width and depth of stock in the item that they specify in and provide high levels of service and expertise. The pricing policy is generally in the medium to high range, depending on factors like the type and exclusivity of merchandise and ownership, that is, whether they are owner operated or a chain operation which has the advantage of bulk purchasing and centralized warehousing system.

a. Catalog merchant
b. Specialty stores
c. Wardrobing
d. Brick and mortar business

27. _________ is a term used in marketing and strategic management to describe a product, service, brand, or company that has such a distinct sustainable competitive advantage that competing firms find it almost impossible to operate profitably in that industry. The existence of a _________ will eliminate almost all market entities, whether real or virtual. Many existing firms will leave the industry, thereby increasing the industry's concentration ratio.

a. 180SearchAssistant
b. Category killer
c. Power III
d. 6-3-5 Brainwriting

28. A _________ is a retail establishment which specializes in selling a wide range of products without a single predominant merchandise line. _________s usually sell products including apparel, furniture, appliances, electronics, and additionally select other lines of products such as paint, hardware, toiletries, cosmetics, photographic equipment, jewelery, toys, and sporting goods. Certain _________s are further classified as discount _________s.

a. 6-3-5 Brainwriting
b. Power III
c. Department store
d. 180SearchAssistant

29. _________ is a form of communication that typically attempts to persuade potential customers to purchase or to consume more of a particular brand of product or service. 'While now central to the contemporary global economy and the reproduction of global production networks, it is only quite recently that _________ has been more than a marginal influence on patterns of sales and production. The formation of modern _________ was intimately bound up with the emergence of new forms of monopoly capitalism around the end of the 19th and beginning of the 20th century as one element in corporate strategies to create, organize and where possible control markets, especially for mass produced consumer goods.

a. ACNielsen
b. Advertising
c. AMAX
d. ADTECH

1. _________ , according to The American Marketing Association, is 'a planning process designed to assure that all brand contacts received by a customer or prospect for a product, service, or organization are relevant to that person and consistent over time.' (Marketing Power Dictionary)

_________ is a term used to describe a holistic approach to marketing. It aims to ensure consistency of message and the complementary use of media. The concept includes online and offline marketing channels.

a. ACNielsen
b. Integrated marketing communications
c. ADTECH
d. AMAX

2. _________ is a form of communication that typically attempts to persuade potential customers to purchase or to consume more of a particular brand of product or service. 'While now central to the contemporary global economy and the reproduction of global production networks, it is only quite recently that _________ has been more than a marginal influence on patterns of sales and production. The formation of modern _________ was intimately bound up with the emergence of new forms of monopoly capitalism around the end of the 19th and beginning of the 20th century as one element in corporate strategies to create, organize and where possible control markets, especially for mass produced consumer goods.

a. Advertising
b. ACNielsen
c. AMAX
d. ADTECH

3. _________ is defined by the American _________ Association as the activity, set of institutions, and processes for creating, communicating, delivering, and exchanging offerings that have value for customers, clients, partners, and society at large. The term developed from the original meaning which referred literally to going to market, as in shopping, or going to a market to sell goods or services.

_________ practice tends to be seen as a creative industry, which includes advertising, distribution and selling.

a. Product naming
b. Customer acquisition management
c. Marketing myopia
d. Marketing

4. _________ refers to messages and related media used to communicate with a market. Those who practice advertising, branding, direct marketing, graphic design, marketing, packaging, promotion, publicity, sponsorship, public relations, sales, sales promotion and online marketing are termed marketing communicators, _________ managers, or more briefly as marcom managers.

a. Marketing communication
b. Merchandising
c. Merchandise
d. Sales promotion

5. _________ involves disseminating information about a product, product line, brand, or company. It is one of the four key aspects of the marketing mix. (The other three elements are product marketing, pricing, and distribution). P>_________ is generally sub-divided into two parts:

- Above the line _________: Promotion in the media (e.g. TV, radio, newspapers, Internet and Mobile Phones) in which the advertiser pays an advertising agency to place the ad
- Below the line _________: All other _________. Much of this is intended to be subtle enough for the consumer to be unaware that _________ is taking place. E.g. sponsorship, product placement, endorsements, sales _________, merchandising, direct mail, personal selling, public relations, trade shows

a. Bottling lines
b. Promotion
c. Davie Brown Index
d. Cashmere Agency

6. _________ is a broad label that refers to any individuals or households that use goods and services generated within the economy. The concept of a _________ is used in different contexts, so that the usage and significance of the term may vary.

A _________ is a person who uses any product or service.

a. 6-3-5 Brainwriting
b. 180SearchAssistant
c. Consumer
d. Power III

7. _________ is the study of when, why, how, where and what people do or do not buy products. It blends elements from psychology, sociology,social psychology, anthropology and economics. It attempts to understand the buyer decision making process, both individually and in groups. It studies characteristics of individual consumers such as demographics and behavioural variables in an attempt to understand people's wants. It also tries to assess influences on the consumer from groups such as family, friends, reference groups, and society in general.

a. Communal marketing
b. Multidimensional scaling
c. Consumer confidence
d. Consumer behavior

8. The _________ is generally accepted as the use and specification of the four p's describing the strategic position of a product in the marketplace. One version of the origins of the _________ starts in 1948 when James Culliton said that a marketing decision should be a result of something similar to a recipe. This version continued in 1953 when Neil Borden, in his American Marketing Association presidential address, took the recipe idea one step further and coined the term 'Marketing-Mix'.

a. Power III
b. Marketing mix
c. 6-3-5 Brainwriting
d. 180SearchAssistant

9. _________ is the process of transforming information from one format into another. The opposite operation is called decoding.

There are a number of more specific meanings that apply in certain contexts:

- _________ is a basic perceptual process of interpreting incoming stimuli; technically speaking, it is a complex, multi-stage process of converting relatively objective sensory input (e.g., light, sound) into subjectively meaningful experience.
- A content format is a specific _________ format for converting a specific type of data to information.
- Character _________ is a code that pairs a set of natural language characters (such as an alphabet or syllabary) with a set of something else, such as numbers or electrical pulses.
- Text _________ uses a markup language to tag the structure and other features of a text to facilitate processing by computers.
- Semantics _________ of formal language A in formal language B is a method of representing all terms (e.g. programs or descriptions) of language A using language B.
- Electronic _________ transforms a signal into a code optimized for transmission or storage, generally done with a codec.
- Neural _________ is the way in which information is represented in neurons.
- Memory _________ is the process of converting sensations into memories.
- Encryption transforms information for secrecy.

.

a. ACNielsen
b. ADTECH
c. Encoding
d. AMAX

10. _________ is the reverse of encoding, which is the process of transforming information from one format into another. Information about _________ can be found in the following:

- Digital-to-analog converter, the use of analog circuit for _________ operations
- Code, a rule for converting a piece of information into another form or representation
- Code (cryptography), a method used to transform a message into an obscured form
- _________
- _________ methods, methods in communication theory for _________ codewords sent over a noisy channel
- Digital signal processing, the study of signals in a digital representation and the processing methods of these signals
- Word _________, the use of phonics to decipher print patterns and translate them into the sounds of language
- deCODE genetics

.

a. Decoding
b. 6-3-5 Brainwriting
c. Power III
d. 180SearchAssistant

11. _________ describes the situation when output from (or information about the result of) an event or phenomenon in the past will influence the same event/phenomenon in the present or future. When an event is part of a chain of cause-and-effect that forms a circuit or loop, then the event is said to 'feed back' into itself.

_________ is also a synonym for:

- _________ Signal; the information about the initial event that is the basis for subsequent modification of the event.
- _________ Loop; the causal path that leads from the initial generation of the _________ signal to the subsequent modification of the event.

_________ is a mechanism, process or signal that is looped back to control a system within itself. Such a loop is called a _________ loop.

a. Feedback
b. 6-3-5 Brainwriting
c. 180SearchAssistant
d. Power III

12. In psychology, philosophy, and the cognitive sciences, _________ is the process of attaining awareness or understanding of sensory information. It is a task far more complex than was imagined in the 1950s and 1960s, when it was predicted that building perceiving machines would take about a decade, a goal which is still very far from fruition. The word _________ comes from the Latin words _________, percepio, meaning 'receiving, collecting, action of taking possession, apprehension with the mind or senses.'

_________ is one of the oldest fields in psychology.

a. Groupthink
b. Power III
c. 180SearchAssistant
d. Perception

13. _________ is one of the four aspects of promotional mix. (The other three parts of the promotional mix are advertising, personal selling, and publicity/public relations.) Media and non-media marketing communication are employed for a pre-determined, limited time to increase consumer demand, stimulate market demand or improve product availability.

a. New Media Strategies
b. Merchandise
c. Sales promotion
d. Marketing communication

14. _________ generally refers to a list of all planned expenses and revenues. It is a plan for saving and spending. A _________ is an important concept in microeconomics, which uses a _________ line to illustrate the trade-offs between two or more goods.

a. 6-3-5 Brainwriting
b. Power III
c. 180SearchAssistant
d. Budget

15. _________ is a sub-discipline and type of marketing. There are two main definitional characteristics which distinguish it from other types of marketing. The first is that it attempts to send its messages directly to consumers, without the use of intervening media.

a. Direct Marketing Associations
b. Database marketing
c. Power III
d. Direct marketing

16. _________ is the practice of managing the flow of information between an organization and its publics. _________ - often referred to as _________ - gains an organization or individual exposure to their audiences using topics of public interest and news items that do not require direct payment. Because _________ places exposure in credible third-party outlets, it offers a third-party legitimacy that advertising does not have.

a. Public relations
b. Graphic communication
c. Symbolic analysis
d. Power III

17. _________ refers to a type of marketing involving the cooperative efforts of a 'for profit' business and a non-profit organization for mutual benefit. The term is sometimes used more broadly and generally to refer to any type of marketing effort for social and other charitable causes, including in-house marketing efforts by non-profit organizations. Cause marketing differs from corporate giving (philanthropy) as the latter generally involves a specific donation that is tax deductible, while cause marketing is a marketing relationship generally not based on a donation.

a. Digital marketing
b. Cause-related marketing
c. Global marketing
d. Diversity marketing

18. _________ refers to marketing strategies applied directly to a specific consumer.

Having the knowledge on the consumer preferences, there are suggested personalized products and promotions to each consumer.

The _________ is based in four main steps in order to fulfill its goals: Those stages are identify, differentiate, interact, and customize.

a. AMAX
b. ACNielsen
c. ADTECH
d. One-to-one marketing

19. A _________ is a type of website, usually maintained by an individual with regular entries of commentary, descriptions of events, or other material such as graphics or video. Entries are commonly displayed in reverse-chronological order. '_________' can also be used as a verb, meaning to maintain or add content to a _________.

a. Blog
b. 6-3-5 Brainwriting
c. Power III
d. 180SearchAssistant

20. _________ is systematic determination of merit, worth, and significance of something or someone using criteria against a set of standards. _________ often is used to characterize and appraise subjects of interest in a wide range of human enterprises, including the arts, criminal justice, foundations and non-profit organizations, government, health care, and other human services.

Depending on the topic of interest, there are professional groups which look to the quality and rigor of the _________ process.

a. Evaluation
b. ADTECH
c. ACNielsen
d. AMAX

21. An _________ is a series of advertisement messages that share a single idea and theme which make up an integrated marketing communication (IMC.) _________s appear in different media across a specific time frame.

The critical part of making an _________ is determining a campaign theme, as it sets the tone for the individual advertisements and other forms of marketing communications that will be used.

a. Advertising campaign
b. ACNielsen
c. AMAX
d. ADTECH

22. Competitiveness is a comparative concept of the ability and performance of a firm, sub-sector or country to sell and supply goods and/or services in a given market. Although widely used in economics and business management, the usefulness of the concept, particularly in the context of national competitiveness, is vigorously disputed by economists, such as Paul Krugman .

The term may also be applied to markets, where it is used to refer to the extent to which the market structure may be regarded as perfectly _________.

a. Competitive
b. Geographical pricing
c. Customs union
d. Free trade zone

23. _________ is speech done on behalf of a company or individual for the intent of making a profit. It is economic in nature and usually has the intent of convincing the audience to partake in a particular action, often purchasing a specific product.

The idea of '_________' was first introduced by the Supreme Court when it upheld Valentine v. Chrestensen (1942).

a. 180SearchAssistant
b. 6-3-5 Brainwriting
c. Power III
d. Commercial speech

24. In marketing a _________ is a ticket or document that can be exchanged for a financial discount or rebate when purchasing a product. Customarily, _________s are issued by manufacturers of consumer packaged goods or by retailers, to be used in retail stores as a part of sales promotions. They are often widely distributed through mail, magazines, newspapers, the Internet, and mobile devices such as cell phones.

a. Merchandising
b. Merchandise
c. Marketing communication
d. Coupon

25. _________ is a branch of philosophy which seeks to address questions about morality, such as how a moral outcome can be achieved in a specific situation (applied _________), how moral values should be determined (normative _________), what moral values people actually abide by (descriptive _________), what the fundamental semantic, ontological, and epistemic nature of _________ or morality is (meta-_________), and how moral capacity or moral agency develops and what its nature is (moral psychology.)

Socrates was one of the first Greek philosophers to encourage both scholars and the common citizen to turn their attention from the outside world to the condition of man. In this view, Knowledge having a bearing on human life was placed highest, all other knowledge being secondary.

a. ADTECH
b. ACNielsen
c. AMAX
d. Ethics

26. _________ is a form of government regulation which protects the interests of consumers. For example, a government may require businesses to disclose detailed information about products--particularly in areas where safety or public health is an issue, such as food. _________ is linked to the idea of consumer rights (that consumers have various rights as consumers), and to the formation of consumer organizations which help consumers make better choices in the marketplace.

a. Federal Bureau of Investigation
b. Sound trademark
c. Trademark dilution
d. Consumer protection

27. False advertising or _________ is the use of false or misleading statements in advertising. As advertising has the potential to persuade people into commercial transactions that they might otherwise avoid, many governments around the world use regulations to control false, deceptive or misleading advertising. Truth in labeling refers to essentially the same concept, that customers have the right to know what they are buying, and that all necessary information should be on the label.

a. Power III
b. Deceptive advertising
c. Misleading advertising
d. Fine print

28. An _________ is a situation that will often involve an apparent conflict between moral imperatives, in which to obey one would result in transgressing another. This is also called an ethical paradox since in moral philosophy, paradox plays a central role in ethics debates. For instance, an ethical admonition to 'love thy neighbour as thy self' is not always just in contrast with, but sometimes in contradiction to an armed neighbour actively trying to kill you: if he or she succeeds, you will not be able to love him or her.

a. ADTECH
b. AMAX
c. ACNielsen
d. Ethical dilemma

29. _________ and viral advertising refer to marketing techniques that use pre-existing social networks to produce increases in brand awareness or to achieve other marketing objectives (such as product sales) through self-replicating viral processes, analogous to the spread of pathological and computer viruses. It can be word-of-mouth delivered or enhanced by the network effects of the Internet. Viral promotions may take the form of video clips, interactive Flash games, advergames, ebooks, brandable software, images, or even text messages.

a. 180SearchAssistant
b. Power III
c. Viral marketing
d. New Media Marketing

30. _________ is the area of applied ethics which deals with the moral principles behind the operation and regulation of marketing. Some areas of _________ overlap with media ethics.

Possible frameworks:

- Value-oriented framework, analyzing ethical problems on the basis of the values which they infringe (e.g. honesty, autonomy, privacy, transparency.) An example of such an approach is the AMA Statement of Ethics.
- Stakeholder-oriented framework, analysing ethical problems on the basis of whom they affect (e.g. consumers, competitors, society as a whole.)
- Process-oriented framework, analysing ethical problems in terms of the categories used by marketing specialists (e.g. research, price, promotion, placement.)

None of these frameworks allows, by itself, a convenient and complete categorization of the great variety of issues in _________.

Contrary to popular impressions, not all marketing is adversarial, and not all marketing is stacked in favour of the marketer.

a. 180SearchAssistant
b. Power III
c. Marketing Ethics
d. 6-3-5 Brainwriting

31. _________ are national trade organizations that seek to advance all forms of direct marketing.

23 direct marketing trade associations from five continents established an International Federation of _________. Founded in 1989, the IFDirect Marketing Associations was established to develop firm lines of communications between direct marketers around the world, and is dedicated to improving the practice and communicating the value of direct marketing; and to promoting the highest standards for ethical conduct and effective self-regulation of the direct marketing community.

a. Direct marketing
b. Power III
c. Database marketing
d. Direct Marketing Associations

1. _________ is a form of communication that typically attempts to persuade potential customers to purchase or to consume more of a particular brand of product or service. 'While now central to the contemporary global economy and the reproduction of global production networks, it is only quite recently that _________ has been more than a marginal influence on patterns of sales and production. The formation of modern _________ was intimately bound up with the emergence of new forms of monopoly capitalism around the end of the 19th and beginning of the 20th century as one element in corporate strategies to create, organize and where possible control markets, especially for mass produced consumer goods.

a. AMAX
b. ADTECH
c. ACNielsen
d. Advertising

2. _________ is one of the four aspects of promotional mix. (The other three parts of the promotional mix are advertising, personal selling, and publicity/public relations.) Media and non-media marketing communication are employed for a pre-determined, limited time to increase consumer demand, stimulate market demand or improve product availability.

a. Merchandise
b. Marketing communication
c. New Media Strategies
d. Sales promotion

3. _________ generally refers to a list of all planned expenses and revenues. It is a plan for saving and spending. A _________ is an important concept in microeconomics, which uses a _________ line to illustrate the trade-offs between two or more goods.

a. Power III
b. 6-3-5 Brainwriting
c. 180SearchAssistant
d. Budget

4. _________ involves disseminating information about a product, product line, brand, or company. It is one of the four key aspects of the marketing mix. (The other three elements are product marketing, pricing, and distribution). P>_________ is generally sub-divided into two parts:

- Above the line _________: Promotion in the media (e.g. TV, radio, newspapers, Internet and Mobile Phones) in which the advertiser pays an advertising agency to place the ad
- Below the line _________: All other _________. Much of this is intended to be subtle enough for the consumer to be unaware that _________ is taking place. E.g. sponsorship, product placement, endorsements, sales _________, merchandising, direct mail, personal selling, public relations, trade shows

a. Cashmere Agency
b. Davie Brown Index
c. Bottling lines
d. Promotion

5. In marketing and advertising, a _________ usually an advertising campaign, is aimed at appealing to. A _________ can be people of a certain age group, gender, marital status, etc. (ex: teenagers, females, single people, etc.)

a. National brand
b. Targeted advertising
c. Brand Development Index
d. Target audience

6. _________ is when advertising is carried out in an informative manner Also, _________ tends to help generate a good reputation.

In some circumstances a business might be required to run _________ as part of resolving a law suit. Tobacco companies are one of the more notable examples of this.

a. ADTECH
b. ACNielsen
c. Out-of-home advertising
d. Informative advertising

7. _________ is a form of social influence. It is the process of guiding people toward the adoption of an idea, attitude, or action by rational and symbolic (though not always logical) means. It is strategy of problem-solving relying on 'appeals' rather than coercion.

a. 6-3-5 Brainwriting
b. 180SearchAssistant
c. Power III
d. Persuasion

8. The business terms _________ and pull originated in the logistic and supply chain management, but are also widely used in marketing.

A _________-pull-system in business describes the move of a product or information between two subjects. On markets the consumers usually 'pulls' the goods or information they demand for their needs, while the offerers or suppliers '_________es' them toward the consumers.

a. Completely randomized designs
b. Push
c. Manufacturers' representatives
d. Gold Key Matching Service

9. A _________ is a plan of action designed to achieve a particular goal.

_________ is different from tactics. In military terms, tactics is concerned with the conduct of an engagement while _________ is concerned with how different engagements are linked.

a. Power III
b. 180SearchAssistant
c. 6-3-5 Brainwriting
d. Strategy

10. In economics, _________ is the desire to own something and the ability to pay for it. The term _________ signifies the ability or the willingness to buy a particular commodity at a given point of time .

.

a. Market dominance
b. Demand
c. Market system
d. Discretionary spending

11. _________ is defined by the American _________ Association as the activity, set of institutions, and processes for creating, communicating, delivering, and exchanging offerings that have value for customers, clients, partners, and society at large. The term developed from the original meaning which referred literally to going to market, as in shopping, or going to a market to sell goods or services.

_________ practice tends to be seen as a creative industry, which includes advertising, distribution and selling.

a. Customer acquisition management
b. Product naming
c. Marketing myopia
d. Marketing

12. _________ is the systematic application of marketing along with other concepts and techniques to achieve specific behavioral goals for a social good. _________ can be applied to promote, for example, merit goods, make the society avoid demerit goods and thus to promote that considers society's well being as a whole. This may include asking people not to smoke in public areas, for example, ask them to use seat belts, prompting to make them follow speed limits.

a. Social marketing
b. Market development
c. Marketing strategy
d. Psychographic

13. An _________ is a situation that will often involve an apparent conflict between moral imperatives, in which to obey one would result in transgressing another. This is also called an ethical paradox since in moral philosophy, paradox plays a central role in ethics debates. For instance, an ethical admonition to 'love thy neighbour as thy self' is not always just in contrast with, but sometimes in contradiction to an armed neighbour actively trying to kill you: if he or she succeeds, you will not be able to love him or her.

a. AMAX
b. ACNielsen
c. ADTECH
d. Ethical dilemma

14. _________ is a branch of philosophy which seeks to address questions about morality, such as how a moral outcome can be achieved in a specific situation (applied _________), how moral values should be determined (normative _________), what moral values people actually abide by (descriptive _________), what the fundamental semantic, ontological, and epistemic nature of _________ or morality is (meta-_________), and how moral capacity or moral agency develops and what its nature is (moral psychology.)

Socrates was one of the first Greek philosophers to encourage both scholars and the common citizen to turn their attention from the outside world to the condition of man. In this view, Knowledge having a bearing on human life was placed highest, all other knowledge being secondary.

a. ADTECH
b. ACNielsen
c. AMAX
d. Ethics

15. _________ is systematic determination of merit, worth, and significance of something or someone using criteria against a set of standards. _________ often is used to characterize and appraise subjects of interest in a wide range of human enterprises, including the arts, criminal justice, foundations and non-profit organizations, government, health care, and other human services.

Depending on the topic of interest, there are professional groups which look to the quality and rigor of the _________ process.

a. ACNielsen
b. AMAX
c. ADTECH
d. Evaluation

16. _________ in organizations and public policy is both the organizational process of creating and maintaining a plan; and the psychological process of thinking about the activities required to create a desired goal on some scale. As such, it is a fundamental property of intelligent behavior. This thought process is essential to the creation and refinement of a plan, or integration of it with other plans, that is, it combines forecasting of developments with the preparation of scenarios of how to react to them.

a. Power III
b. 6-3-5 Brainwriting
c. 180SearchAssistant
d. Planning

17. _________ is a market coverage strategy in which a firm decides to ignore market segment differences and go after the whole market with one offer.it is type of marketing (or attempting to sell through persuasion) of a product to a wide audience. The idea is to broadcast a message that will reach the largest number of people possible. Traditionally _________ has focused on radio, television and newspapers as the medium used to reach this broad audience.

a. Business-to-consumer
b. Marketspace
c. Mass marketing
d. Cyberdoc

18. _________ is a term used to denote a section of the media specifically designed to reach a very large audience such as the population of a nation state. It was coined in the 1920s with the advent of nationwide radio networks, mass-circulation newspapers and magazines, although _________ were present centuries before the term became common. The term public media has a similar meaning: it is the sum of the public mass distributors of news and entertainment across media such as newspapers, television, radio, broadcasting, which may require union membership in some large markets such as Newspaper Guild, AFTRA, ' text publishers.

a. 180SearchAssistant
b. Mass media
c. 6-3-5 Brainwriting
d. Power III

19. _________ is an advertising term for a timing pattern in which commercials are scheduled to run during intervals that are separated by periods in which no advertising messages appear for the advertised item. Any period of time during which the messages are appearing is called a flight, and a period of message inactivity is usually called a hiatus.

The advantage of the _________ technique is that it allows an advertiser who does not have funds for running spots continuously to conserve money and maximize the impact of the commercials by airing them at key strategic times.

a. Consumocracy
b. Strict liability
c. Concession
d. Flighting

20. An _________ is a series of advertisement messages that share a single idea and theme which make up an integrated marketing communication (IMC.) _________s appear in different media across a specific time frame.

The critical part of making an _________ is determining a campaign theme, as it sets the tone for the individual advertisements and other forms of marketing communications that will be used.

a. ADTECH
b. AMAX
c. ACNielsen
d. Advertising campaign

21. The _________ is an independent agency of the United States government, created, directed, and empowered by Congressional statute , and with the majority of its commissioners appointed by the current President.

a. 6-3-5 Brainwriting
b. Power III
c. Federal Communications Commission
d. 180SearchAssistant

22. _________ refers to 'controlling human or societal behaviour by rules or restrictions.' _________ can take many forms: legal restrictions promulgated by a government authority, self-_________, social _________, co-_________ and market _________. One can consider _________ as actions of conduct imposing sanctions (such as a fine.) This action of administrative law, or implementing regulatory law, may be contrasted with statutory or case law.

a. Rule of four
b. Non-conventional trademark
c. CAN-SPAM
d. Regulation

23. _________ is an advertisement in which a particular product specifically mentions a competitor by name for the express purpose of showing why the competitor is inferior to the product naming it.

This should not be confused with parody advertisements, where a fictional product is being advertised for the purpose of poking fun at the particular advertisement, nor should it be confused with the use of a coined brand name for the purpose of comparing the product without actually naming an actual competitor. ('Wikipedia tastes better and is less filling than the Encyclopedia Galactica.')

In the 1980s, during what has been referred to as the cola wars, soft-drink manufacturer Pepsi ran a series of advertisements where people, caught on hidden camera, in a blind taste test, chose Pepsi over rival Coca-Cola.

a. Cost per conversion
b. GL-70
c. Heavy-up
d. Comparative advertising

24. Regulation refers to 'controlling human or societal behaviour by rules or restrictions.' Regulation can take many forms: legal restrictions promulgated by a government authority, self-regulation, social regulation (e.g. norms), co-regulation and market regulation. One can consider regulation as actions of conduct imposing sanctions (such as a fine.) This action of administrative law, or implementing _________ law, may be contrasted with statutory or case law.

a. Robinson-Patman Act
b. Privacy law
c. Right to Financial Privacy Act
d. Regulatory

25. _________ is a broad label that refers to any individuals or households that use goods and services generated within the economy. The concept of a _________ is used in different contexts, so that the usage and significance of the term may vary.

A _________ is a person who uses any product or service.

a. 180SearchAssistant
b. 6-3-5 Brainwriting
c. Power III
d. Consumer

26. _________ as a legal term refers to promotional statements and claims that express subjective rather than objective views, such that no reasonable person would take literally. _________ is especially featured in testimonials.

In a legal context, the term originated in the English Court of Appeal case Carlill v Carbolic Smoke Ball Company, which centred on whether a monetary reimbursement should be paid when an influenza preventative device failed to work.

a. Puffery
b. Conquesting
c. Heinz pickle pin
d. Custom media

27. _________ is a form of government regulation which protects the interests of consumers. For example, a government may require businesses to disclose detailed information about products--particularly in areas where safety or public health is an issue, such as food. _________ is linked to the idea of consumer rights (that consumers have various rights as consumers), and to the formation of consumer organizations which help consumers make better choices in the marketplace.

a. Federal Bureau of Investigation
b. Trademark dilution
c. Sound trademark
d. Consumer protection

28. In marketing a _________ is a ticket or document that can be exchanged for a financial discount or rebate when purchasing a product. Customarily, _________s are issued by manufacturers of consumer packaged goods or by retailers, to be used in retail stores as a part of sales promotions. They are often widely distributed through mail, magazines, newspapers, the Internet, and mobile devices such as cell phones.

a. Merchandise
b. Marketing communication
c. Merchandising
d. Coupon

29. _________ is that part of statistical practice concerned with the selection of individual observations intended to yield some knowledge about a population of concern, especially for the purposes of statistical inference. Each observation measures one or more properties (weight, location, etc.) of an observable entity enumerated to distinguish objects or individuals.

a. Richard Buckminster 'Bucky' Fuller
b. AStore
c. Sports Marketing Group
d. Sampling

30. In the United States consumer sales promotions known as _________ or simply sweeps (both single and plural) have become associated with marketing promotions targeted toward both generating enthusiasm and providing incentive reactions among customers by enticing consumers to submit free entries into drawings of chance (and not skill) that are tied to product or service awareness wherein the featured prizes are given away by sponsoring companies. Prizes can vary in value from less than one dollar to more than one million U.S. dollars and can be in the form of cash, cars, homes, electronics, etc.

_________ frequently have eligibility limited by international, national, state, local, or other geographical factors.

a. Commercial planning
b. Claritas Prizm
c. Market segment
d. Sweepstakes

31. _________s are structured marketing efforts that reward, and therefore encourage, loyal buying behaviour -- behaviour which is potentially of benefit to the firm.

In marketing generally and in retailing more specifically, a loyalty card, rewards card, points card, advantage card, or club card is a plastic or paper card, visually similar to a credit card or debit card, that identifies the card holder as a member in a _________. Loyalty cards are a system of the loyalty business model.

a. 6-3-5 Brainwriting
b. Power III
c. Loyalty program
d. 180SearchAssistant

32. _________ is a form of advertisement, where branded goods or services are placed in a context usually devoid of ads, such as movies, the story line of television shows Broadcasting ' Cable reported, 'Two thirds of advertisers employ 'branded entertainment'--_________--with the vast majority of that (80%) in commercial TV programming.' The story, based on a survey by the Association of National Advertisers, added, 'Reasons for using in-show plugs varied from 'stronger emotional connection' to better dovetailing with relevant content, to targetting a specific group.'

_________ became common in the 1980s, but can be traced back to the nineteenth century in publishing.

a. 6-3-5 Brainwriting
b. 180SearchAssistant
c. Power III
d. Product placement

33. A _________ is an amount paid by way of reduction, return, or refund on what has already been paid or contributed. It is a type of sales promotion marketers use primarily as incentives or supplements to product sales. The mail-in _________ is the most common.

a. Rebate
b. Lifestyle city
c. Personalization
d. Strand

34. _________ are a form of online advertising on the World Wide Web intended to attract web traffic or capture email addresses. It works when certain web sites open a new web browser window to display advertisements. The pop-up window containing an advertisement is usually generated by JavaScript, but can be generated by other means as well.

a. Customer intelligence
b. Power III
c. Project Portfolio Management
d. Pop-up ads

1. _________ consists of the processes a company uses to track and organize its contacts with its current and prospective customers. _________ software is used to support these processes; information about customers and customer interactions can be entered, stored and accessed by employees in different company departments. Typical _________ goals are to improve services provided to customers, and to use customer contact information for targeted marketing.

a. Commercialization
b. Demand generation
c. Customer relationship management
d. Product bundling

2. A _________ is a process that can allow an organization to concentrate its limited resources on the greatest opportunities to increase sales and achieve a sustainable competitive advantage. A _________ should be centered around the key concept that customer satisfaction is the main goal.

A _________ is most effective when it is an integral component of corporate strategy, defining how the organization will successfully engage customers, prospects, and competitors in the market arena.

a. Cyberdoc
b. Societal marketing
c. Psychographic
d. Marketing strategy

3. _________ is defined by the American _________ Association as the activity, set of institutions, and processes for creating, communicating, delivering, and exchanging offerings that have value for customers, clients, partners, and society at large. The term developed from the original meaning which referred literally to going to market, as in shopping, or going to a market to sell goods or services.

_________ practice tends to be seen as a creative industry, which includes advertising, distribution and selling.

a. Product naming
b. Marketing myopia
c. Customer acquisition management
d. Marketing

4. _________ in organizations and public policy is both the organizational process of creating and maintaining a plan; and the psychological process of thinking about the activities required to create a desired goal on some scale. As such, it is a fundamental property of intelligent behavior. This thought process is essential to the creation and refinement of a plan, or integration of it with other plans, that is, it combines forecasting of developments with the preparation of scenarios of how to react to them.

a. Power III
b. Planning
c. 6-3-5 Brainwriting
d. 180SearchAssistant

5. Customer _________ consists of the processes a company uses to track and organize its contacts with its current and prospective customers. CRelationship management software is used to support these processes; information about customers and customer interactions can be entered, stored and accessed by employees in different company departments. Typical CRelationship management goals are to improve services provided to customers, and to use customer contact information for targeted marketing.

a. Product bundling
b. Green marketing
c. Marketing
d. Relationship management

6. A _________ is a plan of action designed to achieve a particular goal.

_________ is different from tactics. In military terms, tactics is concerned with the conduct of an engagement while _________ is concerned with how different engagements are linked.

a. Strategy
b. 6-3-5 Brainwriting
c. 180SearchAssistant
d. Power III

7. A personal and cultural _________ is a relative ethic _________, an assumption upon which implementation can be extrapolated. A _________ system is a set of consistent _________s and measures that is soo not true. A principle _________ is a foundation upon which other _________s and measures of integrity are based.

a. Perceptual maps
b. Supreme Court of the United States
c. Value
d. Package-on-Package

8. A _________ is a collection of symbols, experiences and associations connected with a product, a service, a person or any other artifact or entity.

_________s have become increasingly important components of culture and the economy, now being described as 'cultural accessories and personal philosophies'.

Some people distinguish the psychological aspect of a _________ from the experiential aspect.

a. Store brand
b. Brand
c. Brandable software
d. Brand equity

9. _________ refers to the additional value of a commodity over the cost of commodities used to produce it from the previous stage of production. An example is the price of gasoline at the pump over the price of the oil in it. In national accounts used in macroeconomics, it refers to the contribution of the factors of production, i.e., land, labor, and capital goods, to raising the value of a product and corresponds to the incomes received by the owners of these factors. The factors of production provide 'services' which raise the unit price of a product (X) relative to the cost per unit of intermediate goods used up in the production of X. _________ is shared between the factors of production (capital, labor, also human capital), giving rise to issues of distribution.

a. Power III
b. Consumer spending
c. Deregulation
d. Value added

10. A trade fair (trade show or expo) is an exhibition organized so that companies in a specific industry can showcase and demonstrate their latest products, service, study activities of rivals and examine recent trends and opportunities. Some trade fairs are open to the public, while others can only be attended by company representatives (members of the trade) and members of the press, therefore _________ are classified as either 'Public' or 'Trade Only'. They are held on a continuing basis in virtually all markets and normally attract companies from around the globe.

a. Power III
b. 180SearchAssistant
c. 6-3-5 Brainwriting
d. Trade shows

11. _________ is a method of direct marketing in which a salesperson solicits to prospective customers to buy products or services, either over the phone or through a subsequent face to face or Web conferencing appointment scheduled during the call.

_________ can also include recorded sales pitches programmed to be played over the phone via automatic dialing. _________ has come under fire in recent years, being viewed as an annoyance by many.

a. Joe job
b. Directory Harvest Attack
c. Telemarketing
d. Phishing

12. _________ is the ability of an individual or group to seclude themselves or information about themselves and thereby reveal themselves selectively. The boundaries and content of what is considered private differ among cultures and individuals, but share basic common themes. _________ is sometimes related to anonymity, the wish to remain unnoticed or unidentified in the public realm.

a. 6-3-5 Brainwriting
b. Power III
c. 180SearchAssistant
d. Privacy

13. _________ is a branch of philosophy which seeks to address questions about morality, such as how a moral outcome can be achieved in a specific situation (applied _________), how moral values should be determined (normative _________), what moral values people actually abide by (descriptive _________), what the fundamental semantic, ontological, and epistemic nature of _________ or morality is (meta-_________), and how moral capacity or moral agency develops and what its nature is (moral psychology.)

Socrates was one of the first Greek philosophers to encourage both scholars and the common citizen to turn their attention from the outside world to the condition of man. In this view, Knowledge having a bearing on human life was placed highest, all other knowledge being secondary.

a. AMAX
b. ADTECH
c. ACNielsen
d. Ethics

14. _________ is a form of communication that typically attempts to persuade potential customers to purchase or to consume more of a particular brand of product or service. 'While now central to the contemporary global economy and the reproduction of global production networks, it is only quite recently that _________ has been more than a marginal influence on patterns of sales and production. The formation of modern _________ was intimately bound up with the emergence of new forms of monopoly capitalism around the end of the 19th and beginning of the 20th century as one element in corporate strategies to create, organize and where possible control markets, especially for mass produced consumer goods.

a. AMAX
b. Advertising
c. ACNielsen
d. ADTECH

15. _________ , according to The American Marketing Association, is 'a planning process designed to assure that all brand contacts received by a customer or prospect for a product, service, or organization are relevant to that person and consistent over time.' (Marketing Power Dictionary)

_________ is a term used to describe a holistic approach to marketing. It aims to ensure consistency of message and the complementary use of media. The concept includes online and offline marketing channels.

a. Integrated marketing communications
b. ACNielsen
c. AMAX
d. ADTECH

16. _________ refers to messages and related media used to communicate with a market. Those who practice advertising, branding, direct marketing, graphic design, marketing, packaging, promotion, publicity, sponsorship, public relations, sales, sales promotion and online marketing are termed marketing communicators, _________ managers, or more briefly as marcom managers.

a. Merchandising
b. Sales promotion
c. Merchandise
d. Marketing communication

17. Importance of _________ is critical for any commercial organization. Expanding business is not possible without increasing sales volumes, and effective _________ goal is to organize sales team work in such a manner that ensures a growing flow of regular customers and increasing amount of sales.

The four phase-model of Management Process

1. Conception
2. Planning
3. Execution
4. Control

This model is cyclical, so it is a constant/continuous process.

===_________ is attainment of sales force goals in a effective ' efficient manner through planning, staffing, training, leading ' controlling organizational resources.

a. Hit rate
b. Sales process
c. Sales management
d. Request for proposal

18. In economics, _________ is the desire to own something and the ability to pay for it. The term _________ signifies the ability or the willingness to buy a particular commodity at a given point of time .

.

a. Market system
b. Market dominance
c. Discretionary spending
d. Demand

19. In economics, the _________ can be defined as the graph depicting the relationship between the price of a certain commodity, and the amount of it that consumers are willing and able to purchase at that given price. It is a graphic representation of a demand schedule The _________ for all consumers together follows from the _________ of every individual consumer: the individual demands at each price are added together.

_________s are used to estimate behaviors in competitive markets, and are often combined with supply curves to estimate the equilibrium price (the price at which sellers together are willing to sell the same amount as buyers together are willing to buy, also known as market clearing price) and the equilibrium quantity (the amount of that good or service that will be produced and bought without surplus/excess supply or shortage/excess demand) of that market.

a. Power III
b. 180SearchAssistant
c. 6-3-5 Brainwriting
d. Demand curve

20. _________ is one of the four Ps of the marketing mix. The other three aspects are product, promotion, and place. It is also a key variable in microeconomic price allocation theory.

a. Competitor indexing
b. Price
c. Relationship based pricing
d. Pricing

21. Radio-frequency identification (_________) is the use of an object (typically referred to as an _________ tag) applied to or incorporated into a product, animal, or person for the purpose of identification and tracking using radio waves. Some tags can be read from several meters away and beyond the line of sight of the reader.

Most _________ tags contain at least two parts.

a. 180SearchAssistant
b. Power III
c. 6-3-5 Brainwriting
d. RFID

22. An _________ is the manufacturing of a good or service within a category. Although _________ is a broad term for any kind of economic production, in economics and urban planning _________ is a synonym for the secondary sector, which is a type of economic activity involved in the manufacturing of raw materials into goods and products.

There are four key industrial economic sectors: the primary sector, largely raw material extraction industries such as mining and farming; the secondary sector, involving refining, construction, and manufacturing; the tertiary sector, which deals with services (such as law and medicine) and distribution of manufactured goods; and the quaternary sector, a relatively new type of knowledge _________ focusing on technological research, design and development such as computer programming, and biochemistry.

a. ADTECH
b. AMAX
c. ACNielsen
d. Industry

23. _________ is one of the four growth strategies of the Product-Market Growth Matrix defined by Ansoff. _________ occurs when a company enters/penetrates a market with current products. The best way to achieve this is by gaining competitors' customers (part of their market share.)

a. Pasar pagi
b. Horizontal market
c. Marketization
d. Market penetration

24. _________ involves disseminating information about a product, product line, brand, or company. It is one of the four key aspects of the marketing mix. (The other three elements are product marketing, pricing, and distribution). P>_________ is generally sub-divided into two parts:

- Above the line _________: Promotion in the media (e.g. TV, radio, newspapers, Internet and Mobile Phones) in which the advertiser pays an advertising agency to place the ad
- Below the line _________: All other _________. Much of this is intended to be subtle enough for the consumer to be unaware that _________ is taking place. E.g. sponsorship, product placement, endorsements, sales _________, merchandising, direct mail, personal selling, public relations, trade shows

a. Promotion
b. Bottling lines
c. Davie Brown Index
d. Cashmere Agency

25. _________ is one of the four aspects of promotional mix. (The other three parts of the promotional mix are advertising, personal selling, and publicity/public relations.) Media and non-media marketing communication are employed for a pre-determined, limited time to increase consumer demand, stimulate market demand or improve product availability.

a. Marketing communication
b. Sales promotion
c. New Media Strategies
d. Merchandise

26. _________ is systematic determination of merit, worth, and significance of something or someone using criteria against a set of standards. _________ often is used to characterize and appraise subjects of interest in a wide range of human enterprises, including the arts, criminal justice, foundations and non-profit organizations, government, health care, and other human services.

Depending on the topic of interest, there are professional groups which look to the quality and rigor of the _________ process.

a. ACNielsen
b. AMAX
c. Evaluation
d. ADTECH

27. An _________ is a series of advertisement messages that share a single idea and theme which make up an integrated marketing communication (IMC.) _________s appear in different media across a specific time frame.

The critical part of making an _________ is determining a campaign theme, as it sets the tone for the individual advertisements and other forms of marketing communications that will be used.

a. ADTECH
b. ACNielsen
c. Advertising campaign
d. AMAX

28. The _________, a unit of the United States Department of Labor, is the principal fact-finding agency for the U.S. government in the broad field of labor economics and statistics. The BLS is an independent national statistical agency that collects, processes, analyzes, and disseminates essential statistical data to the American public, the U.S. Congress, other Federal agencies, State and local governments, business, and labor representatives. The BLS also serves as a statistical resource to the Department of Labor.

a. Bureau of Labor Statistics
b. Power III
c. Gross national product
d. Consumer Expenditure Survey

29. _________ is a retail channel for the distribution of goods and services. At a basic level it may be defined as marketing and selling products, direct to consumers away from a fixed retail location. Sales are typically made through party plan, one to one demonstrations, and other personal contact arrangements.

a. 6-3-5 Brainwriting
b. Power III
c. Direct Selling
d. 180SearchAssistant

30. The _________ is the name of several similar trade associations in the United States, United Kingdom, Australia, Malaysia, Singapore, and New Zealand that represent direct selling companies.

The American _________ is the national trade association of leading firms that manufacture and distribute goods and services sold directly to consumers typically through in-home or person-to-person sales.

Founded in Binghamton, New York in 1910, the association was originally called the Agents Credit Association.

a. Power III
b. 180SearchAssistant
c. 6-3-5 Brainwriting
d. Direct Selling Association

31. _________ is a mathematical science pertaining to the collection, analysis, interpretation or explanation, and presentation of data. It also provides tools for prediction and forecasting based on data. It is applicable to a wide variety of academic disciplines, from the natural and social sciences to the humanities, government and business.

a. Null hypothesis
b. Median
c. Type I error
d. Statistics

Chapter 1

1. d	2. d	3. d	4. d	5. d	6. d	7. c	8. b	9. d	10. d
11. a	12. b	13. a	14. d	15. d	16. d	17. c	18. d	19. a	20. d
21. c	22. d	23. d	24. d	25. c	26. c	27. d	28. d	29. d	30. a
31. b	32. d	33. c	34. d	35. d	36. b	37. c	38. b		

Chapter 2

1. d	2. d	3. d	4. d	5. b	6. c	7. b	8. b	9. c	10. c
11. d	12. a	13. c	14. d	15. d	16. b	17. c	18. d	19. a	20. a
21. a	22. c	23. d	24. b	25. c	26. d	27. c	28. d	29. d	30. d
31. d	32. d	33. b	34. d	35. d	36. d	37. d	38. d	39. b	40. d
41. d	42. d	43. d	44. d	45. d	46. d				

Chapter 3

1. a	2. d	3. d	4. a	5. d	6. d	7. a	8. b	9. a	10. a
11. d	12. d	13. d	14. c	15. c	16. a	17. d	18. b	19. c	

Chapter 4

1. b	2. d	3. b	4. d	5. d	6. c	7. a	8. c	9. a	10. c
11. a	12. d	13. d	14. d	15. c	16. b	17. d	18. d	19. d	20. a
21. d	22. c	23. c	24. a	25. d	26. a	27. d			

Chapter 5

1. d	2. c	3. b	4. c	5. b	6. d	7. d	8. d	9. a	10. b
11. a	12. c	13. d	14. b	15. b	16. d	17. a	18. a	19. a	20. a
21. c	22. c	23. d	24. d	25. d	26. d	27. b	28. a	29. b	30. a
31. d	32. c	33. d	34. d	35. b	36. c	37. d			

Chapter 6

1. d	2. d	3. d	4. a	5. d	6. a	7. b	8. b	9. d	10. d
11. a	12. a	13. d	14. d	15. d	16. d	17. d	18. c		

Chapter 7

1. d	2. d	3. c	4. d	5. d	6. b	7. b	8. d	9. b	10. d
11. d	12. b	13. d	14. d	15. c	16. d	17. c	18. a	19. d	20. d
21. a	22. d	23. b	24. b	25. c	26. b	27. d	28. d	29. d	30. d
31. b	32. d	33. b	34. b	35. d	36. c	37. d	38. d	39. b	40. d
41. c	42. c	43. d	44. c						

Chapter 8

1. a	2. a	3. c	4. a	5. d	6. d	7. b	8. c	9. b	10. a
11. d	12. c	13. a	14. d	15. d	16. d	17. a	18. d	19. b	20. a
21. a	22. d	23. d	24. a	25. d					

Chapter 9

1. d	2. a	3. d	4. d	5. d	6. d	7. d	8. d	9. a	10. a
11. d	12. a	13. a	14. b	15. b	16. c	17. a	18. d	19. d	20. d
21. d	22. d	23. b	24. b	25. a	26. b	27. b	28. b	29. d	30. d
31. d	32. d	33. c	34. d						

Chapter 10

1. d	2. b	3. a	4. a	5. b	6. a	7. d	8. d	9. d	10. c
11. d	12. c	13. c	14. d	15. d	16. d	17. a	18. d	19. a	20. c
21. d	22. b	23. d	24. c	25. d	26. d	27. d	28. a	29. d	30. d
31. c	32. d	33. b							

Chapter 11

1. d	2. a	3. b	4. a	5. d	6. d	7. d	8. a	9. c	10. d
11. c	12. c	13. a	14. d	15. d	16. b	17. d	18. c	19. c	20. a
21. d	22. d	23. b	24. c	25. d	26. d	27. b	28. c	29. a	30. d
31. c									

Chapter 12

1. a	2. a	3. a	4. d	5. d	6. c	7. d	8. d	9. d	10. d
11. d	12. a	13. b	14. b	15. c					

Chapter 13

1. d	2. d	3. d	4. a	5. d	6. b	7. b	8. b	9. a	10. d
11. d	12. a	13. b	14. a	15. b	16. d	17. c	18. b	19. b	20. d
21. a	22. d	23. b	24. d	25. a	26. d	27. d	28. d	29. a	30. a
31. a	32. d								

Chapter 14

1. a	2. d	3. b	4. b	5. d	6. c	7. d	8. d	9. b	10. d
11. c	12. a	13. a	14. d	15. d	16. b	17. d	18. d	19. d	20. c
21. a	22. a	23. d	24. d	25. d	26. a	27. d	28. d	29. d	30. d
31. a	32. b	33. a	34. d	35. d	36. d	37. d			

Chapter 15

1. a	2. d	3. c	4. d	5. d	6. b	7. d	8. b	9. d	10. a
11. b	12. d	13. a	14. b	15. d	16. d	17. a	18. d	19. b	20. d
21. a	22. d	23. a	24. d	25. d	26. b				

Chapter 16

1. b	2. d	3. d	4. b	5. a	6. d	7. a	8. b	9. a	10. a
11. d	12. d	13. a	14. c	15. d	16. c	17. d	18. d	19. c	20. d
21. d	22. d	23. d	24. d	25. d	26. b	27. b	28. c	29. b	

Chapter 17

1. b	2. a	3. d	4. a	5. b	6. c	7. d	8. b	9. c	10. a
11. a	12. d	13. c	14. d	15. d	16. a	17. b	18. d	19. a	20. a
21. a	22. a	23. d	24. d	25. d	26. d	27. b	28. d	29. c	30. c
31. d									

Chapter 18

1. d	2. d	3. d	4. d	5. d	6. d	7. d	8. b	9. d	10. b
11. d	12. a	13. d	14. d	15. d	16. d	17. c	18. b	19. d	20. d
21. c	22. d	23. d	24. d	25. d	26. a	27. d	28. d	29. d	30. d
31. c	32. d	33. a	34. d						

Chapter 19

1. c	2. d	3. d	4. b	5. d	6. a	7. c	8. b	9. d	10. d
11. c	12. d	13. d	14. b	15. a	16. d	17. c	18. d	19. d	20. d
21. d	22. d	23. d	24. a	25. b	26. c	27. c	28. a	29. c	30. d
31. d									

www.ingramcontent.com/pod-product-compliance
Lightning Source LLC
Chambersburg PA
CBHW082047230426
43670CB00016B/2808
* 9 7 8 1 4 2 8 8 7 1 2 0 5 *